HIS KINGDOM WAS SEIZED.
BUT HE'S TAKING IT BACK.

KING of GLORY

FROM
THE HOLY SCRIPTURES

TOLD BY
P. D. BRAMSEN

ILLUSTRATED BY
ARMINDA SAN MARTÍN

D1247419

KING OF GLORY
By P. D. Bramsen
Illustrated by Arminda San Martín
Copyright © 2012 ROCK International
All rights reserved.

ISBN 978-0-97987-067-5

A Publication of
ROCK International
  • **R**elief, **O**pportunity & **C**are for **K**ids
  • **R**esources **O**f **C**rucial **K**nowledge
P.O. Box 4766, Greenville, SC 29608
resources@rockintl.org
www.rockintl.org
www.one-god-one-message.com

All book royalties are reinvested in ROCK International projects. To translate KING OF GLORY or other ROCK publications and broadcasts, contact: resources@rockintl.org

ABOUT THE AUTHOR: Paul Dan Bramsen was born in California. He and his wife raised their three children in Senegal, West Africa, a majority Muslim nation on the edge of the Sahara. Bramsen writes for an international audience, creating resources that tell the stories of the biblical prophets in chronological order. His writings include *THE WAY OF RIGHTEOUSNESS* (a 100-episode radio series broadcast in about a hundred languages), and *ONE GOD ONE MESSAGE* (a book [in 12 languages] designed to help truth-seeking skeptics over their obstacles and into a clear understanding of God's story and message.). Bramsen's writings flow from a passion for the Scriptures and a love for God and people. Contact: pb@rockintl.org

ABOUT THE ARTIST: Arminda San Martín of Argentina writes: "Ever since I can remember, I have been drawing. After taking a break to dedicate myself to being a wife and raising my kids, I restarted my career by obtaining a degree in Fine Arts. I worked hard, exploring different techniques in my own country and also in New York, where I lived for a few years in the '90s. After returning to Argentina I had the chance to develop a professional career doing illustrations for many books, mostly related to nature and spirituality. All my God-given skills have been poured into painting *KING OF GLORY*. For me, this project is a dream come true, a once in a lifetime chance. I cannot thank the Lord enough for this opportunity. I'm also grateful to Paul Bramsen, who is not only an inspired writer but an outstanding editor. I thank God for his knowledge and his constant guidance to achieve this final result." Arminda currently works as an illustrator for a number of publishing houses. Contact: armisanmartin@yahoo.com.ar

Printed in Canada

FOR THE GLORY OF THE KING
AND THE BLESSING OF
KIDS OF ALL AGES
IN EVERY NATION

*"Safe? Who said anything about safe?
'Course he isn't safe. But he's good.
He's the King, I tell you."*

— From *The Lion, the Witch, and the Wardrobe* by C.S. Lewis

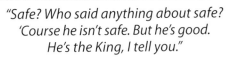

SCENE SELECTION

• Happily Ever After?

• Bad News

• Good News

• Your Response to the King

• Scene Review Questions

• Endnotes

• Going Deeper

BEHIND THE SCENES

A lice was beginning to get very tired of sitting by her sister on the bank, and of having nothing to do; once or twice she had peeped into the book her sister was reading, but it had no pictures or conversations in it, "and what is the use of a book," thought Alice, "without pictures or conversation?"

— Opening lines in *Alice's Adventures in Wonderland* by Lewis Caroll, 1865

The book you are about to read is filled with pictures and conversations, but unlike the classic fantasy story *Alice in Wonderland*,[1] the pictures and conversations in *King of Glory* flow from a story that really happened.[2]

It was with some hesitation that I decided to produce a book with pictures about the greatest story ever told.

Years ago, while living in West Africa, I took a course in radio program production. On the first day of class the professor asked, "What is one of the main advantages radio has over television?" His answer surprised us.

"It provides a better picture."

True.

Even high-budget blockbuster movies struggle to match the ability of the human mind to translate simple words into vivid mental images. The ancient Scriptures of the prophets paint hundreds of word-pictures that no movie can satisfactorily show, that no human artist can fully illustrate.

So I admit it. No artwork can perfectly portray the best story ever told. Still, it has been fun to try.

Arminda San Martín, our gifted and gracious artist from Argentina, has done an amazing and accurate job of translating the biblical stories from words to paint. With digital pen and brush, Arminda completed the preliminary sketches and final paintings in just fourteen months. I hope you will be as thrilled with her work as I am.

Now think about this.

If we read a storybook, where do we begin? In the middle? No, we start at the beginning. Only then will we understand the story. Likewise, to understand the Scriptures, we must start at the beginning and follow the story to its logical and satisfying conclusion.

The writings of the prophets contain hundreds of short stories which all fit together to form one story. In writing *King of Glory*, I have felt somewhat like a florist assigned to go into a vast garden of endless flowers, select a few dozen, and arrange them into a single bouquet that displays the glory of the entire garden. For this book, I have selected a few dozen key stories from the Scriptures and arranged them into a 70-scene drama in an attempt to display the glory of the eternal King who has revealed Himself in human history.

My prayer to God is that the showing and telling of this true story will inspire audiences of all ages to delight in the writings of the prophets, fall in love with the One of whom they speak, and join the happy kingdom that will never end.

For a clear picture,

P. D. Bramsen

Opening

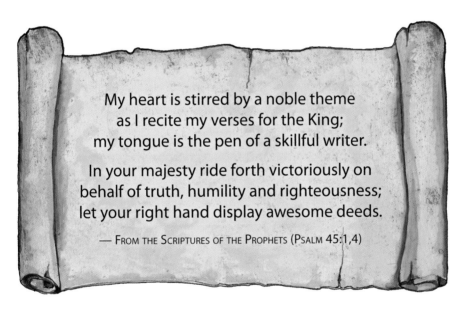

My heart is stirred by a noble theme
as I recite my verses for the King;
my tongue is the pen of a skillful writer.

In your majesty ride forth victoriously on
behalf of truth, humility and righteousness;
let your right hand display awesome deeds.

— From the Scriptures of the Prophets (Psalm 45:1,4)

SCENE 1
THE KING AND HIS KINGDOM

Long, long before the world began, there was a king, the King of glory.

This King was far, far above and beyond anyone or anything you or I could imagine. In the endlessness of eternity He was the only King, and His kingdom the only kingdom, a realm of perfect wisdom, love, joy, and peace. The kingdom had no need of sun or stars, for the King Himself was its light.

While the kingdom was limitless in its size, it was limited in its subjects. Some say the King had no subjects at all.

Or did He?

One of the early mysteries of this King was that even when He alone existed, He was never alone.

Still, He wanted to share His life with other intelligent beings.

So this good and wise King made a heavenly province with millions of dazzling, super-intelligent spirit beings called angels. He knew them all by name and He wanted them to know Him too. Life with the King was non-stop adventure.

But the King wanted more than angels. So He created a realm of time, space, and matter—a mind-boggling universe with a sparkling planet that would become home to a community of amazing creatures called humans.

Different from the angels, the human family began with just two beings, a man and a woman. As with the angels, the King wanted to share His life with them too.

Then something happened, something terrible. Rebellion arose in the kingdom, first in heaven, then on earth.

A rebel angel seized the kingdom of earth by capturing its humans. But the King was not taken by surprise.

Deep in the heart of the King was a rescue plan so great, so mysterious, so extravagant, so far-reaching, that He would take thousands and thousands of years to fulfill it.

What else would you expect from the King of eternity?

He lives above time.

SCENE 2
THE KING AND HIS PROPHETS

To know the King and His plan,
you must know His book.

Over more than 15 centuries the King chose about 40 people to record His story and message. They were called prophets. The King gave them His words, which they wrote on scrolls to be copied, circulated, and kept for future generations. Though most of the prophets never knew each other, their writings tell one consistent story and message.

The writings of the prophets are called the Holy Scriptures. Without the Scriptures we could only guess where we came from, why we are here, and where we are going. To know the correct answers we need the King's book.

About 3,500 years ago, the King inspired a prophet
by the name of Moses to write,

> Man does not live on bread alone but on every word that comes from the mouth of the LORD. (Deuteronomy 8:3)

Today the King's words are collected in one book, *the Holy Bible*. Holy means *pure* or *set apart from all others*. Bible means *book* or *collection of books*. The Bible is the world's best seller and most translated book. Thousands of papyrus and leather scrolls show it to be the best preserved of all ancient texts.[3]

The Scriptures have two main parts.

The first part is the Old Testament (Torah, Psalms, etc.) where the King foretells His plan.

The second part is the New Testament (Gospels, Acts, etc.) where the King fulfills His plan.

Testament means *covenant, contract,* or *agreement*. The Old Testament foretells what God planned to do. The New Testament records the fulfilment of His plan. Only God can write history before it happens.

The difference between the Old and New Testaments is the difference between having a great king send you letters and photos—and having that king come visit you in person.

The Scriptures came first to the Middle East, Africa, Asia, and Europe, then later to the Americas and beyond. The prophets came from the Middle East, but the story and message they wrote is for every nation. For every family. For every person.

For you.

SCENE 3
THE KING AND HIS UNIVERSE

If we could travel back through time and space,

back,

back,

way back,

before there were people, planets, or stars, we would witness the power and glory behind the first words of Scripture:

> In the beginning God created the heavens and the earth. (Genesis 1:1)

Today, many people think the world and its wonders came to exist apart from an all-wise Creator. But their theories do not adequately explain the complex design and predictable order of the universe.

In His book, the King says,

> The heavens declare the glory of God; the skies
> proclaim the work of his hands. (Psalm 19:1)

Speaking of hands, look at your own. Wiggle your thumbs. Try to hold a book, broom, or hammer without them. Notice the fingernails, joints, and skin. Think of some important things you do with your hands. Who but a master craftsman could design such tools?

What kind of wisdom and power would be required to make a billion galaxies? Or to create a living cell with its millions of complex parts? Or knit together the cell's microscopic coiled threads with the genetic codes that make you *you*?

Some three thousand years ago, a prophet and king named David wrote,

> You knit me together in my mother's womb. I praise you
> because I am fearfully and wonderfully made. (Psalm 139:13-14)

Would you like to meet the One who formed you? Would you like to live forever with the Maker and Master of the galaxies? You can. He has revealed Himself. He wants you to know Him. He wants your family and community to know Him too. He invites you to understand His plan, experience His love, behold His majesty, submit to His rule, and live for His glory. But He will not force you to be His subject.

After all, He is not just *a* king. He is *the* King. *The King of glory.*

This is His story.

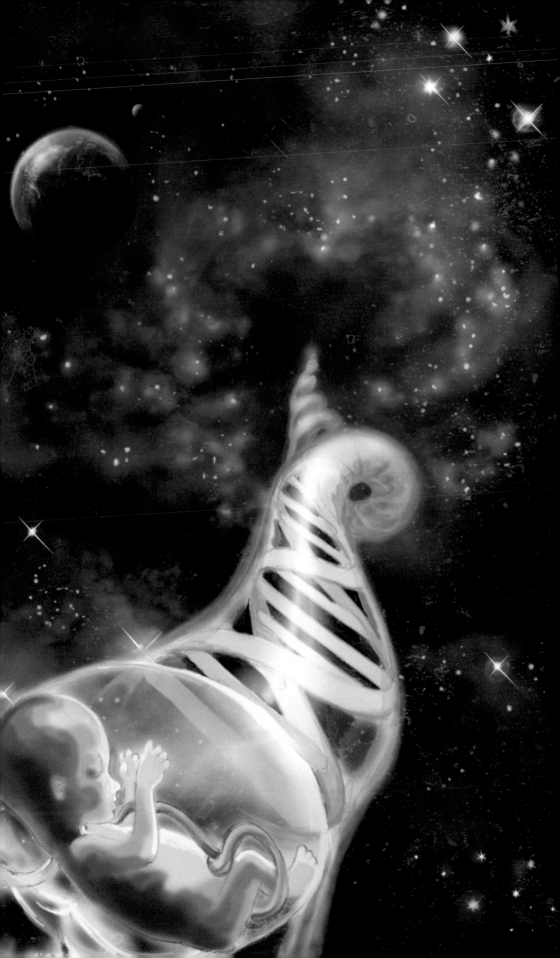

Part 1

THE KING FORETELLS HIS PLAN

— OLD TESTAMENT —

# Scene 4

The First Day

God's book begins in a way worthy of a king. He tells us what He wants us to know and nothing more.

> In the beginning God created the heavens and the earth. (Genesis 1:1)

Everything we can see and touch has a beginning, but the Creator and Owner of the universe has no beginning or end. He is the invisible, eternal Spirit who can be everywhere at once. He sees and knows everything.

Do you know His name? God has many names, but His most famous name is the LORD. In the original language of God's book, His name is *Yahweh*, which means *The One Who IS*, or simply *I AM*.

The creation story continues with the King's description of the original earth.

> Now the earth was formless and empty, darkness was over the surface of the deep, and the Spirit of God was hovering over the waters. (Genesis 1:2)

It was time to prepare the planet for people.

> And God said, "Let there be light," and there was light.

> God saw that the light was good, and He separated the light from the darkness. God called the light "day," and the darkness he called "night." And there was evening, and there was morning—the first day. (Genesis 1:3-5)

What did God do on the first day of creation? He commanded light to pierce the darkness. Later the sun would shine on Earth, but not on Day One. God wants us to know that He is the Source of light.

> God is light; in him there is no darkness at all. (1 John 1:5)

God is pure, like light. He cannot be defiled. Even when light shines on very dirty things, it is pure. God is perfect. God is holy.

Did you notice who was there with God at the creation site? His Holy Spirit was there, hovering over the waters. His Word was there too, speaking.

> In the beginning was the Word, and the Word was with God, and the Word was God. He was with God in the beginning. Through him all things were made .... (John 1:1-3)

The Holy Spirit of God and the Word have always been with the one true God. That is why it can be said of the King:

Even when He alone existed, He was never alone.

SCENE 5

A PERFECT WORLD

In six orderly days, the King created a beautiful, wonderful world. God simply spoke, and perfectly-designed marvels appeared.

On the first day God said, "Let there be light!" and there was light.

On the second day God made Earth's atmosphere with the blue sky we see and the invisible air we breathe. God designed the sky with a perfect mix of life-supporting gases, such as oxygen and nitrogen.

On the third day God said, "Let dry ground appear!" And that is what happened. Then God said, "Let the land produce vegetation!" Instantly, grass, plants, flowers, and fruit began to grow, each with its own seed.

On day four God commanded the sun and moon to shine and to mark Earth's years, months, and days. He also made the stars.

On day five God said, "Let the waters swarm with fish and other life! Let the skies be filled with birds of every kind!" And that is what happened.

On the sixth day God said, "Let the earth bring forth every kind of animal—livestock, small animals, and wildlife!" God made each living creature able to reproduce offspring of the same kind and to care for its young.

God saw that it was good. (Genesis 1:25)

Peace reigned. In the beginning all the animals were friendly. They did not kill and eat each other. The plants supplied their food.

Order reigned. Like clockwork, the sun would keep the right distance from Earth. The moon would change from new moon to full moon. The earth would recycle its air, water, and waste. If ruled well, the kingdom of earth would never lack any good thing. It would be the ideal home for mankind.

Each day of creation gives us a clue as to what God is like.[4]

Day 1 shows us that God is *holy*. He is perfect and pure, like light.
Day 2. God is *all-powerful*. He made and maintains the atmosphere.
Day 3. God is *good*. He created thousands of plants and foods for us.
Day 4. God is *faithful*. The sun and the moon stay in their orbits.
Day 5. God is *life*. He put fish in the sea and birds in the sky.
Day 6. God is *love*. After God created the animals, it was time to form the creatures upon whom He would pour out His love.

It was time to create the special beings who could reflect His holiness, power, goodness, faithfulness, life, and love.

SCENE 6
THE FIRST MAN

On the sixth day of creation, the King conversed within Himself (God, His Holy Spirit, and His Word), saying,

> "Let us make man in our image, in our likeness,[5] and let them rule … over all the earth, and over all the creatures …."

> So God created man in his own image, in the image of God he created him; male and female he created them. (Genesis 1:26-27)

When the Scripture says that God created people in His own image, it does not mean that God is just like us. It means that we are to reflect His nature and personality. As Roman coins were later stamped with the emperor's image, so God's image was stamped on mankind. The first man and woman were created with the ability to think, love, and speak like their Creator so that they could enjoy a close relationship with Him. People were not made to be God's slaves, but God's friends.

In creating humans in His own likeness, God gave them dominion. People were to care for and to rule the earth for God, to discover its secrets and use its resources wisely. Such capacities set mankind apart from the animal kingdom.

To animals, God gave two dimensions: body and soul.
To humans, God gave three dimensions: body, soul, and spirit.

> The LORD God formed the man from the dust of the ground[6] and breathed into his nostrils the breath of life, and the man became a living being. (Genesis 2:7)

The body was merely the house, or tent, into which God breathed man's soul and spirit.

The soul was man's personal intellect, emotions, and will, which made it possible for man to think, feel, and choose.

The spirit connected man to God. While the body equipped man to connect with the visible world, the spirit equipped man to connect with the invisible God. The LORD wanted humans to know Him.

People would be God's special treasure. Since God made them, He was not only their Creator, but also their Owner.

The LORD God named the first man Adam, meaning *Of the Earth*, or simply *Man*. Later God would form the first woman, but before that there were some preparations to make.

Adam needed a home and a job.

SCENE 7
A PERFECT HOME

After making the first human body from dust[6] and breathing life into it, God planted a garden in Eden, somewhere in the Middle East.

A crystal-clear river flowed through the garden.

> And the LORD God made all kinds of trees grow out of the ground—trees that were pleasing to the eye and good for food. In the middle of the garden were the tree of life and the tree of the knowledge of good and evil.
>
> The LORD God took the man and put him in the Garden of Eden to work it and take care of it. (Genesis 2:9,15)

The LORD God did not ask Adam if he wanted to live in Eden. God was man's Creator-Owner. He knew what was best for man.

Adam's garden home was filled with endless delights—things to see, hear, smell, touch, and taste. Sparkling streams. Singing birds. Fragrant flowers. Furry creatures. Juicy fruits. Crunchy vegetables. Sweet berries. Mysterious forests. Colorful rocks. Fascinating bugs. And a trillion other wonders waiting to be discovered.

But man was made for more than exploring and eating. God made Adam to be head of the human race. God wanted Adam and his family to reign with Him forever. But only those who can be trusted with small tasks can be given big tasks.

So God gave Adam his first job: Care for the garden.

This garden was a perfect place. It had no thorns or weeds or bad insects. The climate was ideal and the soil was rich, yet it never rained. Instead, a mist came up from the earth and watered the ground.

God also gave Adam another job: Name the animals.

The LORD brought the creatures to him to see what he would call them. Imagine the scene. A pair of animals with flowing manes and powerful legs gallop up. Adam studies them, strokes their backs, and names them *horses*. At the Creator's call, a huge bird with hooked beak and broad wings swoops down. "Eagle!" says Adam. Next, a beast in an orange coat with black stripes goes by. What do you think Adam called it?

> So the man gave names to all the livestock, the birds in the sky and all the wild animals. (Genesis 2:20)

Eden was the perfect place for man to get to know his Creator.

It was time to give Adam a test.

Scene 8
The Law of Sin and Death

From the start, God and man were friends, but that friendship needed to be tested. The King of the universe would not fill His kingdom with subjects who were forced to submit to Him.

God loved Adam and had awesome plans for him and his future family. Because God wanted people and not puppets, He gave Adam one rule to obey.

> The LORD God commanded the man, "You are free to eat from any tree in the garden; but you must not eat from the tree of the knowledge of good and evil, for when you eat of it you will surely die." (Genesis 2:16-17)

This was not a difficult command. Adam could eat any of the fruits in the garden *except one*. By obeying this simple rule, Adam could show that he trusted his Creator to know what was best for him.

What did God say would happen to Adam if he broke this rule?

Did God tell Adam that if he ate the forbidden fruit he must begin to do religious rituals, use prayer beads, fast, give alms, go to a church, synagogue, or mosque, and try to do enough good deeds to balance out his bad deeds? Is that what God said?

No, that is not what God said.

God told Adam, "When you eat of it you will surely *die*."

Disobedience to God's law is called *sin*.
The penalty for breaking God's rule would be *death*.
In His book, the King calls this "the law of sin and death" (Romans 8:2).

The King's law says that sin must be punished with death.

Death means *separation*. If Adam disobeyed God's one rule, he would become like a broken branch which begins to wither and die the instant it is separated from its source of life.

If Adam decided to do what he wanted to do instead of what the King of the universe told him to do, that would be an act of rebellion; that would be *sin*.

Sin would end man's friendship with God.
Sin would cause man's body to grow old and die.
Sin would separate man's spirit, soul, and body from God forever.

Sin is deadly.

SCENE 9
THE FIRST WOMAN

After God had given the first man a job to do and a rule to obey, it was time to form the first woman.

> The LORD God said, "It is not good for the man to be alone. I will make a helper suitable for him."
>
> So the LORD God caused the man to fall into a deep sleep; and while he was sleeping, he took one of the man's ribs and closed up the place with flesh. Then the LORD God made a woman from the rib he had taken out of the man, and he brought her to the man.
>
> The man said, "This is now bone of my bones and flesh of my flesh; she shall be called 'woman,' for she was taken out of man." (Genesis 2:18, 21-23)

Did you notice who performed the first surgery—and who arranged the first marriage? Yes, it was God.

Woman means *Out of Man*. Later, Adam named his wife Eve, meaning *Mother of All*. While God gave them different roles, He made the man and woman equal in value. Like Adam, Eve was created in the image of God. She too was made to know her Creator-Owner, reflect His character, and enjoy a happy relationship with Him forever.

> God saw all that he had made, and it was very good. And there was evening, and there was morning—the sixth day.
>
> By the seventh day God had finished the work he had been doing; so on the seventh day he rested from all his work. (Genesis 1:31; 2:2)

Why did God rest on the seventh day? Because His work was finished. Also, by creating our world in six days and resting on the seventh, God established the seven-day week—a work-rest cycle still practiced worldwide.

The LORD God cared for Adam and Eve like a wise and loving father. Each evening, He would come into the garden to walk and talk with them. They were happy and comfortable in His presence.

> The man and his wife were both naked, and they felt no shame. (Genesis 2:25)

Imagine a perfect world inhabited by a perfect couple in close friendship with their perfect Creator. That's how things were in the beginning.

What went wrong?

Scene 10

The Kingdom of Light

Before we discover what went wrong on earth,
we need to understand some things about Heaven.

This other world, also called Paradise, is a place of pure light, enchanting colors, thrilling music, satisfying talk, and unfolding mysteries. Heaven's simplest activities surpass earth's greatest pleasures. Heaven is another dimension.

Heaven is the King's home.

The best attraction of this happy place is the King Himself. Every corner of the celestial city is designed to reflect His majesty.

> The city was pure gold, as clear as glass. (Revelation 21:18)

The most detailed description of heaven is recorded in the last book of Scripture, *The Revelation*. God gave the prophet John a look into heaven and told him to write down what he saw.

> There before me was a throne in heaven with someone sitting on it. … A rainbow that shone like an emerald encircled the throne. … From the throne came flashes of lightning, rumblings and peals of thunder. … In front of the throne there was what looked like a sea of glass, clear as crystal.

> Then I looked and heard the voice of many angels, numbering thousands upon thousands, and ten thousand times ten thousand. They encircled the throne … they never stop saying: "Holy, holy, holy is the Lord God Almighty, who was, and is, and is to come." (Revelation 4:2-3,5-6; 5:11; 4:8)

Angel means *messenger* or *servant*. Angels are spirit beings. Like their Creator, angels are invisible to man, except when sent on missions where they need to be seen.

The King of heaven made angels before He made humans. In His book, He tells us that "all the angels shouted for joy" (Job 38:7) as they watched Him create the world.

God gave His angels the capacity to know, obey, praise, and serve Him forever. The angels were not God's slaves. As with humans, God did not force them to submit to Him. He wanted happy, willing servants.

The Scriptures tell of one high-ranking angel to whom God had given great intelligence, beauty, and power.

If you know this angel's story, then you know where evil came from.

The Kingdom of Darkness

L ucifer was one of God's chief angels. His name means *Shining One.* The Scriptures of the prophets describe Lucifer as "the model of perfection, full of wisdom and perfect in beauty" (Ezekiel 28:12).[7]

Then Lucifer started looking at himself instead of on his great Creator-King. For the first time ever, a created thing became proud of itself! Blinded by his own beauty and intelligence, and forgetting who had made him, Lucifer said in his heart,

> "I will raise my throne above the stars of God....
> I will ascend above the tops of the clouds;
> I will make myself like the Most High." (Isaiah 14:13-14)

Lucifer wanted to be king. He wanted *his will* to be done instead of God's will.

Sin had entered the universe.

Lucifer convinced a third of the angels to join his rebellion, but God, who cannot tolerate sin, threw them out of His heavenly home.

Lucifer's name was changed to Satan, meaning *accuser.* He is also called the devil, meaning *deceiver.* The evil angels are called demons.

In a dark secret place, God has prepared a prison for the devil and his demons. That place is called hell and the Lake of Fire. It is a place of eternal separation from God, a place where rebels will cause no more trouble. One day Satan and all his demons will be forever locked up in that prison, but they are not all there yet.

So where did these evil spirits go after God threw them out?

They moved into Earth's atmosphere. There the devil organized his angels in ranks. *If he could not rule in heaven he would rule on earth!* That is why the Scripture calls Satan "the ruler of the kingdom of the air, the spirit who is now at work in those who are disobedient" (Ephesians 2:2).

The devil and his demons are invisible to us, but real. While we do not know what they look like, we do know their dark and evil purpose. They will use all sorts of trickery to get people to join their kingdom of darkness and doom. They will stop at nothing to destroy you.

> Satan disguises himself as an angel of light. (2 Corinthians 11:14 NLT)

> Your enemy the devil prowls around like a roaring lion looking for someone to devour. (1 Peter 5:8)

Now let's get back to the story of our first parents.

Scene 12

The Serpent

Adam and Eve's lives were filled with adventure and purpose.

Each day was full of wonder as they explored their vast garden, cared for its creatures and plants, and sampled its foods.

Each evening was even more wonderful as their Creator-Owner honored them with a personal visit. How they loved to walk and talk with Him! The man and his wife were happy in their garden home.

But Satan was not happy. He hated God and he hated these two creatures who reflected the image of God!

So the devil, who had failed to seize the kingdom of heaven, plotted to take over the kingdom of earth. *If only he could get Adam, the head of the human race, to choose to break God's law. But he would not tempt Adam directly…*

One day Eve heard a voice.

It wasn't Adam. It wasn't God.

It was a serpent!

For Eve, a talking reptile was just another new discovery. She had no idea that God's enemy was using the serpent. Nor did she know Satan wanted to use her to tempt Adam to break God's law.

The serpent had waited patiently, his calculating eyes tracking the woman. Then, at the opportune moment, he hissed out to her,

> "Did God really say, 'You must not eat from any tree in the garden'?" (Genesis 3:1)

Satan wanted Eve to doubt God's word. He also wanted her to think that God was keeping something good from her and her husband.

> The woman said to the serpent, "We may eat fruit from the trees in the garden, but God did say, 'You must not eat fruit from the tree that is in the middle of the garden, and you must not touch it, or you will die.'"

> "You will not surely die," the serpent said to the woman. "For God knows that when you eat of it your eyes will be opened, and you will be like God, knowing good and evil." (Genesis 3:2-5)

What would Eve do?

SCENE 13

THE CHOICE

God had given Adam and Eve freedom to choose between doing His will or their own.

The LORD knew what was best for these special creatures He had made in His own image. He wanted Adam and Eve to trust Him, even when they didn't understand the reasons behind His rule.

Only God could foresee the terrible, far-reaching consequences of evil, which is why He had told Adam,

> "You must not eat from the tree of the knowledge of good and evil, for when you eat of it you will surely die." (Genesis 2:16-17)

But now the serpent had told Eve,

> "You will *not* surely die." (Genesis 3:4)

Who should Eve trust—her Creator or a creature?

This is what happened:

> When the woman saw that the fruit of the tree was good for food and pleasing to the eye, and also desirable for gaining wisdom, she took some and ate it.
>
> She also gave some to her husband,
> who was with her,
> and he ate it. (Genesis 3:6)

She ate it! He ate it!

Eve ate the forbidden fruit because she was deceived by Satan's tricks. Adam ate it because he deliberately chose to go his own way instead of God's way.

Instead of submitting to their holy and loving Creator, mankind had surrendered to the enemy.

Our first parents had sinned.

SCENE 14
SIN AND SHAME

Adam was the appointed head of the human race. It was to him that God had given the command not to eat from the tree of the knowledge of good and evil. It was not until Adam bit into the unlawful fruit that both he and his wife began to feel the dreadful effects of their choice.

> Then the eyes of both of them were opened, and they realized they were naked; so they sewed fig leaves together and made coverings for themselves. (Genesis 3:7)

Burning shame and heart-wrenching guilt flooded their souls. They felt unclean, inside and out.

Sin brought shame.

Before Adam and Eve broke God's law, they were God-conscious and "felt no shame" (Genesis 2:25). They were honored to be with their Creator, to reflect His image, and to be His friends.

But when they ate from the tree of the knowledge of good and evil, they became self-conscious and ashamed.

Shame replaced honor.

They tried to cover their shame with fig leaves, but no amount of self-effort could fix their problem. They were helpless to get rid of the sin that had invaded their souls. They were helpless to restore the honor they had lost.

It was afternoon.

Soon their holy and loving Creator would come for His evening visit. The thought of seeing Him sent shock waves of terror racing through their bodies.

What would He say to them?

What would they say to Him?

SCENE 15

SPIRITUALLY DEAD

Before they disobeyed God, Adam and Eve rejoiced to see their Creator-Friend each time He came to visit them.

Now they were afraid.

> Then the man and his wife heard the sound of the LORD God as he was walking in the garden in the cool of the day, and they hid from the LORD God among the trees of the garden. (Genesis 3:8)

Like disobedient children who try to hide from their parents, Adam and Eve tried to hide from their Creator.

> But the LORD God called to the man, "Where are you?"
>
> He answered, "I heard you in the garden, and I was afraid because I was naked; so I hid."
>
> And God said, "Who told you that you were naked? Have you eaten from the tree from which I commanded you not to eat?"
>
> The man said, "The woman you put here with me— she gave me some fruit from the tree, and I ate it."
>
> Then the LORD God said to the woman, "What is this you have done?"
>
> The woman said, "The serpent deceived me, and I ate." (Genesis 3:9-13)

Why did Adam and Eve want to hide from God? Because they had sinned. Why did they blame others for their sin? Because they were ashamed.

Adam and Eve no longer displayed the holy image of God. Instead of reflecting their Creator's holiness and love, they now reflected the devil's rebellion and pride.

The first couple had become like a branch broken off a living tree. Their sin had broken off their relationship with the King of the universe.

Spiritually, they were dead. Their sin had separated them from the Source of eternal life.

Physically, they were still alive, but the process of growing old had begun. Death's power had invaded their bodies.

And what was the cause of all this death and destruction?

Sin.

SCENE 16
THE CURSE

At the beginning of human history God and man were together. Peace and joy reigned. Then man broke God's law.

On the same day Adam and Eve sinned, God announced some of the far-reaching consequences of their sin.

To the woman He said,

> "With pain you will give birth to children. Your desire will be for your husband, and he will rule over you." (Genesis 3:16)

Before sin entered the scene, Eve rejoiced in her husband's selfless love and care, but now their sin-contaminated natures would add strife and pain to the joys of marriage.

Next, God told the man,

> "Cursed is the ground because of you; through painful toil you will eat of it all the days of your life. It will produce thorns and thistles for you…. By the sweat of your brow you will eat your food until you return to the ground, since from it you were taken; for dust you are and to dust you will return." (Genesis 3:17-19)

Because of their sin, Adam and Eve had lost dominion over the earth. Their world would now include thorns, pain, sadness, sickness, and death.

Some of us are so accustomed to such misery that we accept it as normal. But was it in God's original design for a fragrant rosebush to have vicious thorns? Or for the wonder of childbirth to include intense pain? Or for those created in God's image to grow old and die? No. God did not design the original creation to fight against itself. It was because of man's sin that the earth came under God's curse.

Mankind had sinned and mankind must die.
The law of sin and death required it.

Death is separation. Sin produces three terrible separations:

1. Spiritual Death: Man's spirit separated from God.
2. Physical Death: Man's spirit and soul separated from his body (and from his loved ones).
3. Eternal Death: Man's spirit, soul, and body forever separated from God in the Lake of Fire.[8]

Man had no way to save himself from the curse of sin.

Was there any hope?

Scene 17
The Promise

Satan had stolen the King's special treasure, but the King had a secret plan to buy it back. Because the ransom price the King planned to pay would be so unthinkably high, neither demons nor humans would understand His plan until after it was fulfilled.

On the same day Satan captured the human race, God said to the serpent,

> "Because you have done this, Cursed are you above all the livestock and all the wild animals! You will crawl on your belly and you will eat dust all the days of your life." (Genesis 3:14)

When God created serpents they had legs. Because the serpent was used by Satan to lead humanity into sin, God cursed it to slither on the ground. (Did you know that pythons and boa constrictors have tiny nubs under their skin where they once had legs?) By making snakes the lowest of beasts, God gave the human family a visual reminder that, in His own time, He will crush "that ancient serpent called the devil, or Satan, who leads the whole world astray" (Revelation 12:9).

Then God said to Satan, who had used the serpent,

> "I will put enmity between you and the woman, and between your offspring and hers; he will crush your head, and you will strike his heel." (Genesis 3:15)

This was the first of many prophecies in which God would, little by little, make known His secret plan to rescue people from Satan, sin, and death. But to hide that plan from Satan and his followers, the King put the prophecy in code.

God promised to send to earth a Savior—the *Offspring of a woman*. The Savior would have a human mother, but no human father. He would be known as the Messiah, meaning *the Chosen One*. Satan would strike the Messiah's heel, but the Messiah would crush Satan's head.

What did all this mean? Later the King would make it clear, but for now God had given Adam and Eve a ray of hope.

Thousands of years later, one of the King's prophets would write,

> The people who walk in darkness will see a great light…
> The virgin will conceive a child! She will give birth to a son
> and will call him Immanuel—'God is with us.' (Isaiah 9:1; 7:14 NLT)

The King would ransom[9] His special treasure.
But how much would it cost?

SCENE 18
THE FIRST SACRIFICE

Do you remember what Adam and Eve did after they ate the forbidden fruit? They made coverings of fig leaves.

Did their coverings make them feel comfortable in the presence of their Creator-Judge? No! They felt ashamed and guilty. They had no way to make themselves right with God.

So God did something for them.

> The LORD God made garments of skin for Adam and his wife and clothed them. (Genesis 3:21)

Who made the first animal sacrifice ever? God did.

The LORD killed some animals, made coats of skin, and dressed Adam and Eve. By doing this, God was teaching them some basic lessons about His justice, mercy, and grace.

Let's think about these three important words.

> *Justice.* Look at the dead animals. Why did God sacrifice them? He did it to show Adam and Eve that the law of sin and death must be upheld. Their sin must be punished with death. That is justice.

> *Mercy.* Look at Adam and Eve. Did God put them to death? No. God provided animals to die in their place. This was God's way of punishing their sin without punishing them. That is mercy.

> *Grace.* Now look at Adam and Eve's beautiful clothing. Did these two law-breakers deserve this gift? No, but God showed them kindness by dressing them in the skins of the sacrificed animals. That is grace.

Because of what the LORD did for them, Adam and Eve were happy to be with God again!

The animal blood covered their *sin.* Adam and Eve deserved to die that day, but innocent animals had died in their place.

The animal skin robes covered their *shame.* Once again, Adam and Eve felt comfortable in the presence of God.

Thousands of years later one of God's prophets wrote,

> I am overwhelmed with joy in the LORD my God!
> For he has dressed me with the clothing of salvation
> and draped me in a robe of righteousness. (Isaiah 61:10 NLT)

Only God has a way to make sinners right again.

SCENE 19
BANISHED

When God expelled the rebellious angels from heaven, their doom was sealed. These spirit beings who had lived in the blazing light of heaven had no excuse for their sin. But for sin-contaminated humans, the LORD had a plan to get them back if they would trust Him.

Still, sin has consequences. Just as God put Lucifer and his evil angels out of the heavenly paradise, so now God put the man and his wife out of the earthly paradise.

> After banishing them from the garden, the LORD God stationed mighty angelic beings to the east of Eden. And a flaming sword flashed back and forth, guarding the way to the tree of life. (Genesis 3:24 NLT)

The tree of life was the other special tree in the middle of the garden. Only perfect people could eat from it. Adam and Eve were no longer perfect. They had sinned and must grow old and die.

Our great Creator God is holy. This means He is pure, clean, perfect, and righteous. Because of His holy nature and holy laws, He must punish sin with death—separation from the Source of Life.

Some people think that God is so "great" that He can ignore the laws He Himself has decreed. Imagine a courtroom where the judge refuses to enforce the laws of the land. Would you say that such a judge is *great*? Imagine a football match where the head referee ignores the rules of the game? Would you call him a *great* referee or a *bad* referee?

Satan wanted Eve to believe that her Creator would not enforce His rules, that He would not punish law-breakers with death. But the righteous King and Judge of the universe always keeps His word.

God is great. You can trust Him.

> Your throne is founded on two strong pillars— righteousness and justice. Unfailing love and truth walk before you as attendants. (Psalm 89:14 NLT)

See if you can answer this riddle: *What can Satan and humans do that the LORD God cannot do?*

Here is God's own answer:

> "I will not break my covenant; I will not take back a single word…. In my holiness I cannot lie." (Psalm 89:34-35 NLT)

The King of the universe cannot go back on His word.

Scene 20
The First Children

Outside the garden, the world was still a beautiful place, but it also included bad things like prickly thorns, pesky bugs, skinned knees, and stuffy noses. Many animals were no longer friendly. Food was not easy to find. Adam and Eve had to work hard just to fill their hungry stomachs.

They also had moments of happiness and joy.

> Adam lay with his wife Eve, and she became pregnant and gave birth to Cain. She said, "With the help of the LORD I have brought forth a man." (Genesis 4:1)

Eve named the world's first baby Cain, meaning *possession*. What a precious treasure from God! Perhaps she thought her son would be the promised Savior, but she soon discovered her cute little boy was stubborn and self-centered—just like his parents!

Later, when their second son was born, Eve named him Abel, meaning *vanity* or *nothing*. Clearly, Adam and Eve could not produce the sinless *Offspring of a woman* who would save people from their sins.

Instead of reflecting God's holy image, Adam and Eve's offspring reflected their own sin-bent natures.

> Adam…had sons and daughters…in his own likeness, in his own image. (Genesis 5:4,3)

Look at the picture. Do you see Cain grabbing the melon from his little brother? He is acting like his parents, who took the fruit that was not theirs. Like a contagious disease, Adam and Eve's sin had infected their children.

> When Adam sinned, sin entered the world. Adam's sin brought death, so death spread to everyone, for everyone sinned. (Romans 5:12 NLT)

An African proverb says, *A rat can only produce offspring that dig.* An Arab proverb voices the same fact: *The son of a duck is a floater.*

When our first parents sinned, they became like a branch broken from a tree. Just as every twig and leaf on the broken branch is affected, so every member of Adam's family branch is affected by Adam's sin.

Long after Adam died, the prophet King David wrote,

> I was born a sinner—yes, from the moment my mother conceived me. (Psalm 51:5 NLT)

We may not like to hear this, but we know it is true.

SCENE 21
SINNERS WORSHIP

Adam and Eve had many sons and daughters, but the Scriptures focus on the story of their first two boys.

> Now Abel kept flocks, and Cain worked the soil. (Genesis 4:2)

Both Cain and Abel were good workers.
Both knew about their Creator.
Both wanted God to accept them and their worship.
Both had the same problem: *Sin.*

Not only were they born sinners, but they lived like sinners. Each day they thought, spoke, and acted in ways that did not reflect God's pure and loving nature. In His book, the King of the universe calls this sin.

> Everyone has sinned; we all fall short of God's glorious standard.
> (Romans 3:23 NLT)

Was there a way for God to pardon Cain and Abel and declare them righteous in His sight? Yes, but it would be very, very costly.

> Without the shedding of blood there is no forgiveness. (Hebrews 9:22)

That unbreakable law of the universe—the law of sin and death—must be carried out. Sin must be punished with death. That is why the King's way of forgiveness required a death payment. While the sinner deserved to die, God would accept the blood of certain kinds of animals, such as a lamb.

The lamb could not be sick or scratched or dirty. It had to be healthy and clean. It had to be a perfect lamb.

The lamb would be killed and burned. It would die in the place of the guilty sinner. The lamb would be the sinner's substitute.

One day both brothers brought offerings to God, but only one brought the right offering.

> In the course of time Cain brought some of the fruits of the soil as an offering to the LORD.

> But Abel brought fat portions from some of the firstborn of his flock. (Genesis 4:3-4)

Which offering do you think God accepted?

SCENE 22
THE LAW OF THE SIN OFFERING

L ook at the brothers. Look at what they are about to offer to God. Look at the altars.

An altar was a raised platform, usually made from stones or dirt. It was a place of death. The altar held up the offering between heaven and earth, between God and man. Whatever was offered on the altar was to be burned with fire.

God always upholds justice but wants to show mercy. How could He do both? How could He punish sin without punishing the sinner?

Long after the time of Cain and Abel, God told the prophet Moses:

> The life of a creature is in the blood, and I have given it to you to make atonement for yourselves on the altar; it is the blood that makes atonement for one's life. (Leviticus 17:11)

> He is to lay his hand on the head of the burnt offering, and it will be accepted on his behalf to make atonement for him. (Leviticus 1:4)

What does *atonement* mean? It has to do with paying the required ransom price so that sins can be covered, cleansed, and forgiven. In Old Testament times, God told people that He would accept the shed blood of healthy lambs, rams, goats, bulls, and doves as payment for their sins. Such blood would provide atonement—a covering for sin—but only until the day God provided a perfect sacrifice to pay the true price required by the law of sin and death.

Now look at Cain and what he is about to offer to God. What a beautiful selection of fruits and vegetables! How hard he had worked to produce this offering! But it could not cover his sins because it had no blood, no death payment.

Look at Abel and his offering. What a sad sight! The little lamb is bound and about to die. Do you see Abel laying his hand on the lamb's head? Because Abel believed God's plan, God took all of Abel's sins and put them on the lamb. Abel is thanking the LORD that although he, Abel, deserves the death penalty, God will accept the lamb's blood as a covering for sin.

God's law required that all sinners be punished with death, but God, in His justice and mercy, would accept the death of a lamb in their place. God calls this "the law of the sin offering" (Leviticus 6:25).

The law of the sin offering set Abel free from the law of sin and death.

But what about Cain?

SCENE 23

ACCEPTED AND REJECTED

D o you see Cain's altar? What is on it? Wilting crops. Now look at Abel's altar. What is on it? Blood and ashes.

What did God think of these two brothers and their worship?

> The LORD looked with favor on Abel and his offering, but on Cain and his offering he did not look with favor. (Genesis 4:4-5)

We are not told how God showed His approval of Abel's sacrifice and His rejection of Cain's sacrifice.[10] The Scripture simply says:

> By faith Abel offered God a better sacrifice than Cain did. By faith he was commended as a righteous man, when God spoke well of his offerings. (Hebrews 11:4)

Because he trusted in the LORD and His plan, Abel was forgiven and declared righteous. This was God's gift to Abel.

God had loaded Abel's sins onto the lamb. The lamb had died in Abel's place. The lamb's blood had been shed and its body burned to ashes. God's righteous anger against sin had fallen on the lamb instead of on Abel. Why was God pleased with Abel's sacrificed lamb? Because it pointed to the coming Savior who would one day pay off the sin debt of the world.

Because of his faith in God's plan Abel was now in a right relationship with God. Later, when Abel died, instead of being forever separated from God, he would go to be with God, who was now his Friend. The law of the sin offering had triumphed over the law of sin and death.

Cain approached God with his prayers, but he ignored God's law that says sin must be punished with death. Cain was religious, but he was not in a right relationship with God. The law of sin and death still hung over him like a dark cloud. If he did not trust God and His plan, he would never know God as his Friend. He would face God as his Judge.

Some people try to defend Cain by saying, "Cain was a farmer. He brought what he had." But God didn't want what he had. Cain could have traded some crops for one of Abel's lambs, or he could have placed his hand on Abel's lamb and worshiped at the same altar.

What would Cain do?

Would he repent and come to God with the right offering?

SCENE 24

THE FIRST MURDER

The LORD had refused Cain's offering. Yet God still loved him and urged him to repent.

What does it mean to repent?

Suppose you want to travel to a certain city. After getting on a train, you realize you boarded the wrong train. What do you do? You admit your error, get off that train, and get on the right train. That is what it means to repent.

To repent means to *change your mind; to turn from what is false and submit to what is true.* To repent before God does not mean that I must punish myself for my sins. It does mean that I must see my sin as God sees it.

God wanted Cain to repent—to stop trusting in his own way and to trust and follow God's way.

> So Cain was very angry, and his face was downcast.
>
> Then the LORD said to Cain, "Why are you angry? Why is your face downcast? If you do what is right, will you not be accepted? But if you do not do what is right, sin is crouching at your door; it desires to have you, but you must master it." (Genesis 4:5-7)

Cain was too proud to repent. *He had been shamed by his brother! He would rid himself of this shame and restore honor in his own way!*

> Now Cain said to his brother Abel, "Let's go out to the field." And while they were in the field, Cain attacked his brother Abel and killed him.
>
> Then the LORD said to Cain, "Where is your brother Abel?"
>
> "I don't know," he replied. "Am I my brother's keeper?"
>
> The LORD said, "What have you done? Listen! Your brother's blood cries out to me from the ground." (Genesis 4:8-10)

Abel's soul and spirit had gone to be with the LORD, but his body would return to dust until a future day when God transforms that dust into a glorious body fit for eternity.

As for Cain, God gave him another chance to repent, but he refused.

> So Cain went out from the LORD's presence. (Genesis 4:16)

In a spirit of rebellion and pride, Cain moved east and built a city. He and his wife had many children. Their great-great-great-great grandchildren made the first metal tools and musical instruments.

Cain's descendants were very intelligent, but they did not know the LORD.

Scene 25

Patience and Judgment

Ten long generations after Adam first sinned,
God gave this sad report on the human family:

> The wickedness of man was great on the earth, and … the
> thoughts of his heart [were] only evil all the time. (Genesis 6:5)

But one family on earth still trusted God.

> Noah found favor in the eyes of the LORD.

> So God said to Noah, "I am going to put an end to all people,
> for the earth is filled with violence because of them. I am surely
> going to destroy both them and the earth. So make yourself
> an ark of cypress wood; make rooms in it and coat it with pitch
> inside and out. This is how you are to build it …." (Genesis 6:8,13-15)

This spacious three-level barge, one and a half times the length
of a football field, would have enough room to house a pair of
each animal species and seven pairs of animals for sin offerings.
The ark would have a ventilation system and one big door.

For a whole century, Noah built the ark, together with his wife,
his three sons and their wives. As he worked, Noah warned the
world of God's coming judgment, but people just mocked him.

Finally the ark was ready. Noah's family had stocked it with supplies.
God brought the animals, reptiles, insects, and birds. What a sight as
they entered the ark, and settled into its thousands of compartments!

Noah and his family entered too. Did anyone else come into
the place of safety? No. So God shut the door. Angry clouds
enveloped the globe, lightning flashed, and thunder crashed.

> On that day all the springs of the great deep burst forth, and
> the floodgates of the heavens were opened. And rain fell on
> the earth for forty days and forty nights. (Genesis 7:11-12)

It was the worst natural disaster in history. Except for
eight souls sheltered in the ark, all humanity perished.
A proud, unbelieving world learned the truth too late.

Geological and fossil records affirm the biblical record.
From the Sahara to the Himalayas, marine fossils can be
unearthed in the world's great deserts and mountains.

In His mercy God is patient, but in His justice He will judge sin.

SCENE 26

A FRESH START

So what happened to Noah and his family, and the animals in the ark? They were saved from God's judgment.

> God remembered Noah and all the wild animals and the livestock that were with him in the ark, and he sent a wind over the earth, and the waters receded. (Genesis 8:1)

The huge ark floated down, finally resting on Ararat, a massive double-peaked mountain in eastern Turkey.

Three times Noah sent out a dove to see if it could find dry ground. The first time the dove just came back. The second time the dove returned to Noah with an olive leaf in its beak. The third time the dove did not return. It had found a home! Noah knew it was time to exit the ark. A whole year had passed since the flood began.

Do you know the first thing Noah did after his family and the animals came out of the ark?

> Noah built an altar to the LORD and, taking some of all the clean animals and clean birds, he sacrificed burnt offerings on it. The LORD smelled the pleasing aroma…. (Genesis 8:20-21)

God's justice and mercy had not changed. Sin still required a death payment. That is why Noah shed the blood of innocent creatures and burned their bodies on an altar, suspended between heaven and earth, between God and man. Such sacrifices pointed to the sinless Messiah who would one day come to earth to provide the real payment for sin.

Next, God gave a command to Noah and his family:

> "Be fruitful and increase in number and fill the earth." (Genesis 9:1)

The LORD God also made a covenant with Planet Earth:

> "I have set my rainbow in the clouds, and it will be the sign of the covenant between me and the earth. … Never again will the waters become a flood to destroy all life." (Genesis 9:13,15)

As a symbol of His covenant, God unveiled a glorious rainbow towering up into the cloudy sky. God promised that He would never again send a global flood.

The rainbow reminds us that, whether to punish or to protect, God always keeps His promises.

Always.

SCENE 27
THE TOWER OF PRIDE

Even when blessed with a fresh start, within a few generations most people had turned away from the LORD to go their own way. For example, God had commanded mankind to spread out and "fill the earth" (Genesis 1:28; 9:1). So what did man do?

The Scripture tells us.

> Now the whole world had one language and a common speech.
>
> As men moved eastward, they found a plain in Shinar [present-day Iraq] and settled there. They said to each other, "Come, let's make bricks and bake them thoroughly."
>
> They used brick instead of stone, and tar for mortar.
>
> Then they said, "Come, let us build ourselves a city, with a tower that reaches to the heavens, so that we may make a name for ourselves and not be scattered over the face of the whole earth." (Genesis 11:1-4)

Instead of praising the great name of the LORD, the builders of this city wanted people to praise them. Like Satan, they were controlled by a spirit of pride and rebellion.

By wanting to build "a tower that reaches to the heavens," they were like religious people today who hope to reach heaven by their own efforts. Like Cain, these people were religious, but they ignored God's way of forgiveness and righteousness. They did not trust God and His plan.

So the LORD God said,

> "Come, let's go down and give them different languages. Then they won't be able to understand each other."
>
> In that way, the LORD scattered them all over the earth; and that ended the building of the city. That is why the city was called Babel, because it was there that the LORD confused the people by giving them many languages, thus scattering them across the earth. (Genesis 11:7-9 NLT)

By giving each family or clan a different language, the LORD stopped their building project. The people had no choice but to move away from Babel and fill the earth, just as God had commanded.

The people did not finish their tower, but God's plans were right on schedule.

SCENE 28
GOD CALLS ABRAHAM

Ten generations had passed since the time of the prophet Noah. Satan had a solid grip on the nations, or so it seemed.

Instead of trusting in the LORD, people trusted in their religions. Some nations worshiped the sun instead of the One who made it. Others bowed to the moon.

The year was about 1925 BC.

In a land northeast of Arabia lived an elderly man named Abram. Later God changed his name to Abraham, meaning *Father of a multitude*.

Abraham was 75 years old. Sarah, his wife, was 65 and childless. Their parents and neighbors were idolators, worshiping created things instead of the Creator.

One day the LORD said to Abraham,

> "Leave your country, your people and your father's household and go to the land I will show you.

> "I will make you into a great nation and I will bless you; I will make your name great, and you will be a blessing. I will bless those who bless you, and whoever curses you I will curse; and all peoples on earth will be blessed through you." (Genesis 12:1-3)

The LORD wanted to make a covenant with Abraham. If he would leave his father's family and go to an unknown land, then the LORD would do two great things with him:

1. God would make Abraham the father of a great nation.
2. Through that new nation, God would bless people in every nation.

If Abraham would trust and follow the LORD, he would become the father of a nation from which would come the prophets, the Scriptures, and the Savior of the world.

What did Abraham do?

> By faith Abraham, when called to go to a place he would later receive as his inheritance, obeyed and went, even though he did not know where he was going. (Hebrews 11:8)

It was not easy for Abraham and his wife to leave their relatives and turn their backs on the family religion. Yet they chose to endure the criticism of their community in order to follow the one true God.

To trust and obey God is not always easy, but it is always best.

SCENE 29
THE PROMISE KEEPER

braham and his wife were old and had no children. Yet the LORD had promised to make Abraham the father of a great nation.

How did Abraham react to God's "impossible" promise?

> Abraham believed God, and it was credited to him as righteousness, and he was called God's friend. (James 2:23; Genesis 15:6)

Like all of Adam's descendants, Abraham was a sinner, but like Abel and Noah, Abraham offered sin offerings to God. Because Abraham believed the LORD and His promises, God credited righteousness to Abraham's record in heaven, and gave him the gift of eternal life. Sarah also trusted in the LORD, and God declared her righteous too.

But it's hard to wait.

After they had been in the land of Palestine for ten years, hoping and praying that Sarah would get pregnant, they decided to "help" God fulfill His promise to give Abraham a son. Following a local custom, Sarah gave her Egyptian maid Hagar to Abraham. He slept with Hagar and she got pregnant and gave birth to a son. They named him Ishmael.

About 13 years later, when Abraham was 99 and Sarah 89, Almighty God appeared to them again. He told them that they would have a son and call him Isaac. The LORD also told Abraham,

> As for Ishmael… I will surely bless him… But my covenant I will establish with Isaac, whom Sarah will bear to you by this time next year." (Genesis 17:20-21)

A year later, Sarah gave birth to Isaac, the son of the promise.

Look at the picture. Do you see Abraham and his wife looking up into the night sky? They are thanking the LORD for His faithfulness. Later, Hagar and Ishmael were sent away, but God was good to them too.

> God was with the boy as he grew up in the wilderness of Paran. He became an expert archer, and his mother arranged a marriage for him with a young woman from Egypt. (Genesis 21:20-21 NLT)

Ishmael became the father of the mighty Arab people, whom God has blessed in so many ways.

As for Isaac, he remained at home, caring for his father's cattle and flocks. Sometimes Isaac helped his father select a healthy lamb, kill it, and burn it on an altar for their sins. But neither Isaac nor his father could imagine the sacrifice God was about to require.

SCENE 30
THE ULTIMATE TEST

God planned to use Abraham and his son to set before the world some prophecies and pictures of His plan to rescue sinners from sin and death. God also planned to test Abraham's faith to the extreme by asking him to do something dreadful, something that would not make sense until the test was over.

At this stage in his life Abraham had absolute trust in the LORD. Abraham knew God. Abraham knew that God is good and just. Yet, would Abraham be able to trust and obey Him, even if what God asked him to do seemed wrong?

Here is the story, straight from the Scriptures:

Some time later, God tested Abraham.

He said to him, "Abraham!"

"Here I am," he replied.

Then God said, "Take your son, your only son, Isaac, whom you love, and go to the region of Moriah.[11] Sacrifice him there as a burnt offering on one of the mountains I will tell you about."

Early the next morning Abraham got up and saddled his donkey. He took with him two of his servants and his son Isaac. When he had cut enough wood for the burnt offering, he set out for the place God had told him about.

On the third day Abraham looked up and saw the place in the distance. He said to his servants, "Stay here with the donkey while I and the boy go over there. We will worship and then we will come back to you."

Abraham took the wood for the burnt offering and placed it on his son Isaac, and he himself carried the fire and the knife.

As the two of them went on together, Isaac spoke up and said to his father Abraham, "Father?"

"Yes, my son?" Abraham replied.

"The fire and wood are here," Isaac said, "but where is the lamb for the burnt offering?"

Abraham answered, "God himself will provide the lamb for the burnt offering, my son."

And the two of them went on together. (Genesis 22:1-8)

Scene 31

The Condemned Son

Did you hear what Abraham told his servants before he and his son climbed the mountain of sacrifice?

"We will worship and then we will come back to you."

How could Abraham's son *come back* if he was to be killed and his body burned? The Scripture says,

Abraham reasoned that God could raise the dead. (Hebrews 11:19)

God had promised to make Isaac the father of a new nation (through which the promised Savior would come). God cannot lie. For Abraham, that was enough.

Meanwhile, what was Isaac thinking? He knew he was a sinner and that he deserved to die for his sins. He also knew that God would accept a substitute. *But today they were going to a place of sacrifice without a ram or a lamb? It made no sense!* So Isaac said to his dad,

"The fire and wood are here, but where is the lamb for the burnt offering?"

Abraham answered, "God himself will provide the lamb for the burnt offering, my son."

Now let's continue the story.

When they reached the place God had told him about, Abraham built an altar there and arranged the wood on it. He bound his son Isaac and laid him on the altar, on top of the wood.

Then he reached out his hand and took the knife to slay his son.

But the angel of the LORD called out to him from heaven, "Abraham! Abraham!"

"Here I am," he replied.

"Do not lay a hand on the boy," he said. "Do not do anything to him. Now I know that you fear God, because you have not withheld from me your son, your only son." (Genesis 22:9-12)

Abraham and his son rejoiced! But what about the required sacrifice?

Abraham looked up and there in a thicket he saw a ram caught by its horns. (Genesis 22:13)

Abraham's son would be spared the death penalty.

God had provided a substitute!

SCENE 32
PICTURES AND PROPHECIES

How did God rescue Abraham's condemned son? He provided a blemish-free, innocent animal to die in his place.

> Abraham looked up and there in a thicket he saw a ram caught by its horns. He went over and took the ram and sacrificed it as a burnt offering instead of his son. (Genesis 22:13)

All these events pictured God's plan to send to earth a holy Savior who would satisfy the requirements of the law of sin and death, and rescue sinners from every nation on earth.

> So Abraham called that place *The LORD Will Provide*. And to this day it is said, "On the mountain of the LORD it will be provided." (Genesis 22:14)

Why did Abraham name the mountain *The LORD **Will** Provide* instead of *The LORD **Has** Provided*?

Had not God just provided a ransom?

By naming the mountain *The LORD **Will** Provide*, the prophet Abraham was foretelling the day when, on this same mountain, God Himself would provide a Sacrifice with blood so costly that God would accept it as full payment for the sin debt of the world, so that whoever believes in that Sacrifice will not perish, but have eternal life.

Some 1,900 years after the prophet Abraham offered the ram on the altar, the promised Savior Himself would look back to this historic event and say,

> "Your father Abraham rejoiced at the thought of seeing my day; he saw it and was glad." (John 8:56)

As the smoke of the ram rose heavenward, God gave Abraham a glimpse of a future burnt offering that would be sacrificed on this same mountain ridge. Suddenly Abraham's answer to his son's question "Where is the lamb?" took on a deeper meaning.

> "God himself will provide *the lamb* for the burnt offering, my son."
> (Genesis 22:8)

For Abraham and his son, God had not yet provided the lamb. He had provided a ram.

Where was *the Lamb*?

At the right time, God Himself would provide the answer.

SCENE 33
A FAITHFUL AND HOLY GOD

Do you remember the two big promises the LORD made to Abraham? First God had said:

"I will make you into a great nation." (Genesis 12:2)

God kept His word. Abraham had Isaac, Isaac had Jacob, and Jacob had twelve sons whose families became the twelve tribes of Israel. God also said:

"All peoples on earth will be blessed through you." (Genesis 12:3)

God would keep that part of His promise too. By working with this special—and often rebellious—nation, God wanted to show all people on earth what He is like and how sinners can come to Him. Whenever God protected this nation, He was protecting His plans to bless you and me—for it was from this nation that the prophets, the Holy Scriptures, and the promised Savior would come.

God's secret plan was moving forward.

Around 1500 BC, God called Moses, a descendant of Abraham, to be His prophet. Moses wrote the first five books of the Bible. God also used Moses to lead Abraham's three million descendants away from four centuries of slavery. God Himself guided them through the hostile desert with a pillar of cloud to provide shade during the day, and with a pillar of fire to provide light at night. By His mighty arm, He opened a path of escape for them in the Red Sea, gave them bread from heaven and water from a rock, and brought them to Mount Sinai.

There at the base of the mountain God told the people,

"You will be for me a kingdom…and a holy nation!" (Exodus 19:6)

God wanted this nation to be holy: set apart for Him and distinct from the nations around them. But the people did not understand what it meant to be holy. They did not see themselves as helpless sinners. They thought they could somehow earn God's favor. To teach them a lesson about His burning anger against sin, the LORD came down in an earth-shaking display of blazing fire and blasting trumpet.

Mount Sinai was covered with smoke, because the LORD descended on it in fire. The smoke billowed up from it like smoke from a furnace, the whole mountain trembled violently, and the sound of the trumpet grew louder and louder. Then Moses spoke and the voice of God answered him." (Exodus 19:18-19 NLT)

God had given Adam one rule.

He was about to give this new nation ten.

SCENE 34
THE TEN COMMANDMENTS

Most of the people in the nation thought they were good enough to be God's people. So the LORD gave them Ten Commandments, first in a thundering voice from Mount Sinai, then on two stone tablets.

Let's read the Ten Commandments (on right, condensed from Exodus 20).

God told Moses that they must obey all ten rules perfectly.

> "Cursed is the man who does not uphold the words of this law."
> (Deuteronomy 27:26)

How do you think the people felt after they heard these ten commands? Do you think they still thought they were good enough? How about you? Do you think you are good enough to live in God's perfect kingdom?

Read again *rule number one*. Do you always put God first? If not, you have failed to keep this law. Read *number five*. If you have ever disobeyed your father or mother, you are guilty before God. Now look at *rule eight*. If you have ever taken something that is not yours or cheated on an exam, you have broken this law. Have you ever told a lie? Then you have not obeyed *rule number nine*. *The last commandment* tells us it is wrong even to want to have what belongs to someone else. God sees the sin in our hearts.

How many sins did it take to ruin Adam and Eve's relationship with God? *Just one.* God's perfect standard has not changed.

> Whoever keeps the whole law and yet stumbles at just
> one point is guilty of breaking all of it. (James 2:10)

God is holy and cannot ignore sin. How would you like to share a room with the rotting body of a dead pig? That is what our sin is like to God. Just as spraying perfume on the stinking body would not cleanse the room, so no amount of religious efforts can cleanse our hearts.

Like a mirror that shows me the dirt on my face, God's law shows me the sin in my heart. Just as the mirror cannot clean my face, so the Ten Commandments cannot cleanse my heart.

> No one will be declared righteous in his sight by observing the law;
> rather, through the law we become conscious of sin. (Romans 3:20)

No matter how good we think we are, we are not good enough to live with God in heaven.

We need a Savior.

1. You shall have no other gods before me.

2. You shall not make for yourself an idol ... for I am the Lord your God.

3. You shall not misuse the name of the Lord your God.

4. Remember the Sabbath day by keeping it holy.

5. Honor your father and your mother.

6. You shall not murder.

7. You shall not commit adultery.

8. You shall not steal.

9. You shall not give false testimony against your neighbor.

10. You shall not covet your neighbor's wife ... or anything that belongs to your neighbor.

# Scene 35

More Pictures

The Ten Commandments gave the new nation a clear standard of right and wrong. That was a good thing. But God's Law also brought bad news. It showed the people that they were in big trouble. Because of their sins they must all die and be separated from God.

The good news was that the LORD would still accept the shed blood of lambs, bulls, goats, and doves to cover their sins. And so, on the same day that God thundered out His Ten Commandments, God told Moses,

"Make an altar… and sacrifice on it your burnt offerings." (Exodus 20:24)

Do you see Moses with his hand on the lamb's head? Do you see people reaching out their hands towards the lamb? Because they believe God and His way of forgiveness, their sins are being put on the innocent lamb. The lamb would then be killed on the altar. The shed blood would cover the sins of the people. Next, the animal's body would be burned to ashes. The ashes would show the people what God had done with their sins. They were forgiven!

But this system of offering animal blood for the forgiveness of sins was only a picture of what God really required.

The sacrifices under the old system were repeated again and again, year after year, but they were never able to provide perfect cleansing for those who came to worship. If they could have provided perfect cleansing, the sacrifices would have stopped, for the worshipers would have been purified once for all time, and their feelings of guilt would have disappeared.

But just the opposite happened. Those yearly sacrifices reminded them of their sins year after year. For it is not possible for the blood of bulls and goats to take away sins. (Hebrews 10:1-4 NLT)

Animals were not created in God's image.

The value of a lamb is not equal to the value of a man. Just as you cannot take a toy car to a car dealer and offer it as payment for a real car, so the blood of a lamb could not pay the high price required by the law of sin and death.

A better sacrifice was needed.

While animal sacrifices could not take away the sin debt of the world, they gave sinners a picture of the One who could.

SCENE 36
MORE PROPHECIES

As the time for the Savior's arrival got closer and closer, the LORD told His prophets to write many more prophecies[12] about this Messiah-King. Here are a few of those ancient promises:

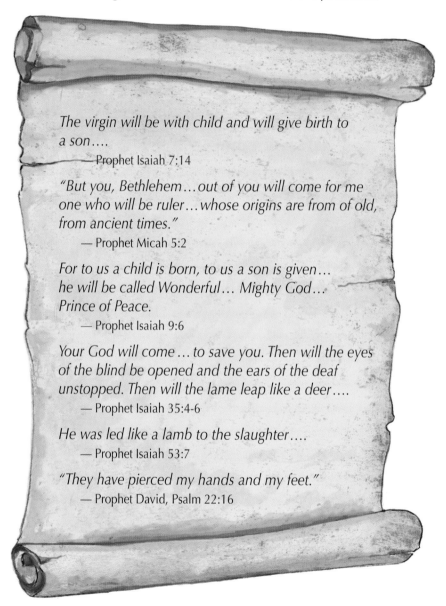

The virgin will be with child and will give birth to a son....
— Prophet Isaiah 7:14

"But you, Bethlehem...out of you will come for me one who will be ruler...whose origins are from of old, from ancient times."
— Prophet Micah 5:2

For to us a child is born, to us a son is given... he will be called Wonderful... Mighty God... Prince of Peace.
— Prophet Isaiah 9:6

Your God will come ... to save you. Then will the eyes of the blind be opened and the ears of the deaf unstopped. Then will the lame leap like a deer....
— Prophet Isaiah 35:4-6

He was led like a lamb to the slaughter....
— Prophet Isaiah 53:7

"They have pierced my hands and my feet."
— Prophet David, Psalm 22:16

The promised Savior was coming!
But when? And who would He be?
How would these prophecies be fulfilled?

Part 2

THE KING FULFILLS HIS PLAN

— NEW TESTAMENT —

THE KING'S STORY CONTINUES

How did you like the first part of the King's book? What did you learn from the Old Testament?

Testament means *agreement or covenant*. Long before God gave the New Testament Scriptures, He said,

> "The time is coming ... when I will make a *new* covenant."
> (Jeremiah 31:31)

In the first covenant with His people, God gave them many laws to show them His holiness and their sinfulness. He also gave them many pictures and prophecies about the coming Savior. In the old covenant the prophets foretold: The Messiah-King *will* come. But in the new covenant we read: The Messiah-King *has* come!

The New Testament contains the *Gospel*. In the Arabic language it is called the *Injil*. Both words mean *Good News*. The Gospel begins with these words:

> This is a record of the ancestors of Jesus the Messiah, a descendant of King David and of Abraham: Abraham was the father of Isaac. Isaac was the father of Jacob.... (Matthew 1:1-2 NLT)

Name by name, the Scriptures register an unbroken chain of descendants from Abraham to Jesus. God would keep His promise to bless all nations by sending the Savior through Abraham's family line.

The New Testament contains four gospel books. Why four? Why not just one? In the Old Testament, God told Moses,

> "The facts of the case must be established by the testimony of two or three witnesses." (Deuteronomy 19:15 NLT)

To confirm His story and message, God chose, not just two or three, but four people to write four separate reports about the Messiah's life. Their names are Matthew, Mark, Luke, and John. Like four news reporters covering the same event, each tells the same story, but from four different viewpoints.

The New Testament has 27 books in all. The book of Acts, written by Luke, tells what happened after the Messiah finished His mission. God inspired Paul (a former terrorist), James and Jude (Jesus' half brothers), and Peter and John (fishermen) to write the rest of the New Testament. Each book reveals more and more about the King and His plans for all who love Him.

Here now is the rest of His story.

SCENE 38
MARY'S STORY

It was time. After thousands of years of preparation, God was about to send the promised Savior-Messiah-King into the world. But who would He be? And how would He come?

> In the time of Herod king of Judea… God sent the angel Gabriel to Nazareth, a town in Galilee, to a virgin pledged to be married to a man named Joseph, a descendant of David. The virgin's name was Mary.
>
> The angel said to her, "Do not be afraid, Mary, you have found favor with God. You will be with child and give birth to a son, and you are to give him the name Jesus. He will be great and will be called the Son of the Most High. The Lord God will give him the throne of his father David, and he will reign… his kingdom will never end."
>
> "How will this be," Mary asked the angel, "since I am a virgin?"
>
> The angel answered, "The Holy Spirit will come upon you, and the power of the Most High will overshadow you. So the Holy One to be born will be called the Son of God." (Luke 1:5,26-27,30-35)

Why did Gabriel call Jesus "the Son of God"?

Some people think this term means that God took a wife and fathered a son. That is *not* what it means. If you are from the continent of Africa, some may call you a "son of Africa." Does this mean Africa got married and had a child? No! It means you come from Africa.

The Messiah is called the Son of God because He came from God. He came into Adam's sin-ruined family but did not originate from it. He is the very Word, Soul, and Son of God.

> In the beginning the Word already existed. He was with God, and he was God. He was in the beginning with God. He created everything there is. Nothing exists that he didn't make. … So the Word became human and lived here on earth among us. He was full of unfailing love and faithfulness. And we have seen his glory, the glory of the only Son of the Father. (John 1:1-3,14 NLT)

Do you remember the promise God made on the day Adam ate the forbidden fruit? God had announced that *the Offspring of a woman* would *crush the Serpent's head*.

That promised Offspring was now in the womb of a virgin girl.

How He would crush the Serpent's head remained to be seen.

SCENE 39
JOSEPH'S STORY

Mary had been pledged in marriage to Joseph, a carpenter living in Nazareth, a border town in northern Palestine.

Both Mary and Joseph were Jews, tracing their ancestry to King David and on back to Abraham. Joseph would have been the crown prince, but his country was ruled by Rome. Roman soldiers patrolled the streets. Jews suspected of treason were arrested and crucified. Tax collectors robbed the people. Life was bitter.

But Joseph was excited. Soon he would take Mary to be his wife. He worked hard to prepare a place where they could live together after the wedding. Then one day he learned the shocking news: Mary was pregnant.

How do you think Joseph felt? It appeared that Mary had been unfaithful to him.

Joseph was heartbroken, but he wanted to do the right thing. So he decided to break the engagement quietly, because he did not want to put Mary to shame.

> As he considered this, he fell asleep, and an angel of the Lord appeared to him in a dream.
>
> "Joseph, son of David," the angel said, "do not be afraid to go ahead with your marriage to Mary. For the child within her has been conceived by the Holy Spirit. And she will have a son, and you are to name him Jesus, for he will save his people from their sins."
>
> All of this happened to fulfill the Lord's message through his prophet: "Look! The virgin will conceive a child! She will give birth to a son, and he will be called Immanuel (meaning, God is with us)." (Matthew 1:20-23 NLT)

Joseph's grief turned to joy. *What an honor! Mary would be the mother of the promised Messiah! And he, Joseph, would be the child's legal guardian!*

The holy Messiah would have a human mother, but no human father. His name would be Jesus, meaning *The LORD Saves*, or simply, *Savior*.

> When Joseph woke up, he did what the angel of the Lord commanded. He brought Mary home to be his wife, but she remained a virgin until her son was born. And Joseph named him Jesus. (Matthew 1:24-25 NLT)

The hand of God was in the whole thing.

SCENE 40
THE ARRIVAL

Seven hundred years earlier, the prophet Micah had foretold that the Messiah-King would be born in Bethlehem, the ancient hometown of King David.

But there was a problem. Mary and Joseph lived in Nazareth, a three-day journey to the north. How would the Scriptures be fulfilled?

God had everything under control.

As the time approached for Mary to give birth, the Roman Emperor Caesar Augustus issued a decree that all subjects of the empire must return at once to the city of their ancestors to register to pay taxes. So Joseph and a very-pregnant Mary traveled from Nazareth to Bethlehem.

> While they were there, the time came for the baby to be born, and she gave birth to her firstborn, a son.
>
> She wrapped him in cloths and placed him in a manger, because there was no room for them in the inn. (Luke 2:6-7)

There in Bethlehem, overcrowded with weary travelers (in town for the tax registration), the promised *Offspring of a woman* was born. The Gospel records the event with precision:

> She gave birth to her firstborn, a son. (Luke 2:6)

On His mother's side, this baby was the newborn son of Mary, but on His Father's side, He was the eternal Son of God. The same Word by which God created the world, the same Voice which thundered from fiery Mount Sinai could now be heard in a baby's soft cry.

And where was He born?

Not in the palace of a king, not in a hospital, not even in a wayside inn. The King from heaven was born where baby lambs are born—in a barn, with a feeding trough for His bed.

It was all part of God's plan.

> For you know the grace of our Lord Jesus Christ, that though he was rich, yet for your sakes he became poor, so that you through his poverty might become rich. (2 Corinthians 8:9)

But couldn't God have arranged some sort of celebration to honor the arrival of His Son?

He did.

SCENE 41

THE SHEPHERDS' STORY

To whom did God first make known the news of the Messiah's coming to earth? To the emperor? The rich and famous? The religious leaders?

No.

The first to receive the electrifying news were poor shepherds, men who raised lambs to be sacrificed on the temple altar in Jerusalem.

> There were shepherds living out in the fields, keeping watch over their flocks at night. An angel of the Lord appeared to them, and the glory of the Lord shone around them, and they were terrified.
>
> But the angel said to them, "Do not be afraid. I bring you good news of great joy that will be for all the people. Today in the town of David a Savior has been born to you; he is Christ[13] the Lord! This will be a sign to you: You will find a baby wrapped in cloths and lying in a manger."
>
> Suddenly a great company of the heavenly host appeared with the angel, praising God and saying, "Glory to God in the highest, and on earth peace to men on whom his favor rests!"
>
> When the angels had left them and gone into heaven, the shepherds said to one another, "Let's go to Bethlehem and see this thing that has happened, which the Lord has told us about."
>
> So they hurried off and found Mary and Joseph, and the baby, who was lying in the manger.
>
> When they had seen him, they spread the word concerning what had been told them about this child, and all who heard it were amazed at what the shepherds said to them. (Luke 2:8-18)

What a story the shepherds had to tell!

The Savior is born! We saw Him! We touched Him! The angel told us He is Christ the LORD! A choir of angels filled the sky! The night was like day! The Messiah has come! He is here! He is here!

Some people believed the shepherds' message. Most did not. But believe it or not, the King, whose birthday split world history in two,[14] had joined the human race.

> Eight days later, when the baby was circumcised, he was named Jesus, the name given him by the angel even before he was conceived. (Luke 2:21 NLT)

SCENE 42

THE MAGI'S STORY

After Jesus' birth in the barn, Joseph arranged to have proper lodging for his little family.

One day some excited Magi (wise men who study the stars) arrived in Jerusalem. Led by a special star, these men had come from faraway Persia in search of the newborn King.

These wise men had one question and one purpose:

"Where is the one who has been born king of the Jews? We saw his star in the east and have come to worship him."

When King Herod heard this he was disturbed, and all Jerusalem with him. When he had called together all the … teachers of the law, he asked them where the Christ was to be born.

"In Bethlehem in Judea," they replied, "for this is what the prophet has written …."

Then Herod called the Magi secretly … and said, "Go and make a careful search for the child. As soon as you find him, report to me, so that I too may go and worship him."

After they had heard the king, they went on their way, and the star they had seen in the east went ahead of them until it stopped over the place where the child was.

When they saw the star, they were overjoyed.

On coming to the house, they saw the child with his mother Mary, and they bowed down and worshiped him. Then they opened their treasures and presented him with gifts of gold and of incense and of myrrh.

And having been warned in a dream not to go back to Herod, they returned to their country by another route.

When they had gone, an angel of the Lord appeared to Joseph in a dream. "Get up," he said, "take the child and his mother and escape to Egypt. Stay there until I tell you, for Herod is going to search for the child to kill him." (Matthew 2:1-13)

Herod tried to murder the child. The people of Jerusalem ignored Him. But the Magi, who crossed a scorching desert to find Him, worshiped Him and gave Him gifts fit for a king: gold, incense, and a costly spice for embalming the dead. Why the embalming spice?

Did these wise men know that Jesus had been born to die?

SCENE 43

THE PERFECT CHILD

After the angel's warning, Joseph took Mary and the child Jesus to Egypt, where they lived as refugees until the death of cruel King Herod.

> After Herod died, an angel of the Lord appeared in a dream to Joseph in Egypt and said, "Get up, take the child and his mother and go to the land of Israel, for those who were trying to take the child's life are dead." (Matthew 2:19-20)

This fulfilled another ancient prophecy spoken by the LORD:

> Out of Egypt I called my son. (Hosea 11:1)

So Joseph and Mary took Jesus to Nazareth, where He grew up along with His half brothers and sisters.[15]

In many ways the boy Jesus was like other children. He ate, slept, played, studied, and learned a trade. But in other ways, Jesus was different from other kids. He was never selfish. He always honored His parents. He never lied. He always pleased His Father in heaven.

> He was holy, blameless, pure, set apart from sinners. (Hebrews 7:26)

Jesus is the only perfect child in history. *Perfect* does not mean He never had a skinned knee or a pimple. It means He had a perfect nature. He was perfectly holy and good. He was also perfect in power and wisdom, but before entering Mary's womb He imposed on Himself certain limitations so that He might live as a human among humans.

> Jesus grew in wisdom and stature, and in favor with God and man.
> (Luke 2:52)

When Jesus was 12 years old He traveled with His parents from Nazareth to Jerusalem for the annual Feast of the Sacrifice, known as the Passover.[16] While His boyhood friends explored the big city, Jesus spent the week in the temple courtyard, sitting among the teachers, listening to them and asking them questions.

> All who heard him were amazed at his understanding and his answers.
> (Luke 2:47 NLT)

The temple was the place where lambs were burned on an altar for the sins of the people. The boy Jesus understood what the scholars did not.

He had come to offer the last Lamb.

SCENE 44
THE LAMB OF GOD

Thirty years had passed since Jesus' birth in Bethlehem. Caesar Augustus was dead; his stepson Caesar Tiberius reigned over the Roman Empire. Herod Antipas ruled in Galilee. Pontius Pilate governed in Judea. And a new prophet was preaching in Palestine.

> In those days John the Baptist came, preaching in the Desert of Judea and saying, "Repent, for the kingdom of heaven is near."
>
> This is he who was spoken of through the prophet Isaiah: "A voice of one calling in the desert, 'Prepare the way for the Lord, make straight paths for him.'"
>
> John's clothes were made of camel's hair, and he had a leather belt round his waist. His food was locusts and wild honey. (Matthew 3:1-4)

While many people of his day dressed in fine silk and ate the best food, John lived simply. He was a man on a mission.

John was the King's forerunner.

Hundreds of years earlier, two prophets, Isaiah and Malachi, wrote about a future prophet who would announce the Messiah-King's arrival. John was that prophet.

While the previous prophets had prophesied: *At the right time, the promised Savior will come to earth*, John preached: *That time has come. The Savior is here!*

Crowds streamed into the desert to hear John. Those who confessed their condition as sinners in need of the Savior were baptized in the Jordan River. In this way they showed their faith in the Messiah, who would wash away their great debt of sin and clothe them in His righteousness.

Day after day, week after week, John spoke to the people about the long-awaited Savior from heaven, "whose sandals I am not fit to carry. He will baptise you with the Holy Spirit" (Matthew 3:11).

Then one day, the Savior came—over the hill, through the crowd, and down to where John was baptizing.

John pointed to Jesus and said,

> "Look, the Lamb of God, who takes away the sin of the world!"
> (John 1:29)

Why did John call Jesus the Lamb of God?

If you know why, then you know the King's mission.

SCENE 45

THE PERFECT SON

Jesus asked John to baptize Him. John objected because the Messiah-King who came from heaven had no need to repent.

> Jesus replied, "Let it be so now; it is proper for us to do this to fulfill all righteousness." (Matthew 3:15)

So John baptized Jesus. By being baptized, Jesus showed that He belonged to the human family He had come to rescue.

> As soon as Jesus was baptized, he went up out of the water. At that moment heaven was opened, and he saw the Spirit of God descending like a dove and lighting on him. And a voice from heaven said, "This is my Son, whom I love; with him I am well pleased!" (Matthew 3:16-17)

As on the first day of creation, God's complex unity is again revealed. Even as God, His Spirit, and His Word worked as one to create the world, so now they would work as one to save it.[17]

We see *the Spirit of God* (who in the beginning was hovering over the waters) come upon Jesus. We watch *the Son of God* (the Word who created the world) walk up out of the river. We hear *the Father* speaking from heaven.

Over the past 30 years, Jesus had lived in obscurity, out of the public eye, but His Father in heaven had observed His every thought, word, and action. And what was God's verdict on His Son's life?

> "With him I am well pleased!"

In all human history, Jesus is the only one who did everything God requires. Everything. Always. Perfectly.

Jesus did what Adam failed to do: reflect the image of God. But Jesus did more than reflect it. He was it.

> In the past God spoke to our forefathers through the prophets at many times and in various ways, but in these last days he has spoken to us by his Son, whom he appointed heir of all things, and through whom he made the universe. The Son is the radiance of God's glory and the exact representation of his being, sustaining all things by his powerful word…. (Hebrews 1:1-3)

No wonder Jesus would later say,

> "I and the Father are one." (John 10:30)

Jesus is the perfect Son.

Scene 46
The Second Man

Satan was not happy that this perfect Man was living in *his* kingdom! But the devil had a strategy. Just as he had tempted the first man to sin, so now he would try to get this Man to sin.

Satan wanted to bring Jesus under his control even as he had brought Adam under his control. If the Son of God could be enticed to sin, then He would not be qualified to save His people from their sin.

> Then Jesus was led by the Spirit into the desert to be tempted by the devil. After fasting for forty days and forty nights, he was hungry.
>
> The tempter came to him and said, "If you are the Son of God, tell these stones to become bread." (Matthew 4:1-3)

Jesus was hungry, but He did not obey the devil. He would not act outside His Father's will. He would not use His infinite power to satisfy His human desires. To combat the devil, Jesus quoted from the Torah of Moses:

> "It is written: 'Man does not live on bread alone, but on every word that comes from the mouth of God.'" (Matthew 4:4; Deuteronomy 8:3)

In his stupid pride, the devil tried again to tempt the Holy One.

> The devil took him to a very high mountain and showed him all the kingdoms of the world and their splendor. "All this I will give you," he said, "if you will bow down and worship me." (Matthew 4:8-9)

When Adam sinned, mankind lost the right to rule the earth. Satan had stolen the dominion of the world, making himself its king. Now the King of glory was on earth to take back the dominion, but He would not do it by bowing to the one He had come to crush.

> Jesus said to him, "Away from me, Satan! For it is written: 'Worship the Lord your God, and serve him only.'" (Matthew 4:10)

Finally, the devil left Jesus. Satan had never tempted anyone like Him, a man who had no desire or capacity to sin. Jesus was different from Adam and his descendants.

> The first man was of the dust of the earth,
> the second man from heaven. (1 Corinthians 15:47)

Adam was the first perfect man. Jesus was the second perfect man.

When Satan tempted Adam to sin, Adam lost and Satan won. When Satan tried to get Jesus to sin, Satan lost and Jesus won.

The first man led us into Satan's kingdom of sin and death. The Second Man came to lead us out.

SCENE 47

THE MESSIAH-KING

After Satan's futile attempts to get Him to sin, Jesus returned to Nazareth, where He had grown up and had worked as a carpenter.

On the Sabbath day he went into the synagogue,
as was his custom. (Luke 4:16)

The synagogue was a house of worship where the Scriptures were read and explained every Saturday. On this particular Saturday Jesus had an announcement to make.

He stood up to read.

The scroll of the prophet Isaiah was handed to him.
Unrolling it, he found the place where it is written:

"The Spirit of the Lord is on me, because he has anointed me to preach good news to the poor. He has sent me to proclaim freedom for the prisoners and recovery of sight for the blind …." (Luke 4:17-18)

What Jesus read in the Scriptures was an ancient prophecy about the Messiah-King who would show the world what God is like and rescue sinners from the dominion of Satan, sin, death, and hell.

Then [Jesus] rolled up the scroll, gave it back to the attendant and sat down.

The eyes of everyone in the synagogue were fastened on him, and he began by saying to them, "Today this scripture is fulfilled in your hearing!" (Luke 4:20-21)

How did Jesus' neighbors react to His claim to be the Messiah who came from heaven to fulfill what the prophets had written in the Scriptures?

All the people in the synagogue were furious when they heard this.
They got up, drove him out of the town, and took him
to the brow of the hill on which the town was built,
in order to throw him down the cliff.

But he walked right through the crowd and went on his way.
(Luke 4:28-30)

Jesus had dominion. Unlike Adam's sin-infected and dying descendants, the Messiah-King anointed[18] by God was in perfect control.
No one could touch Him unless He allowed it.

But He would touch them.

Scene 48

Dominion over Demons and Disease

In the Scriptures of the prophets, one of the Messiah's titles is *The Arm of the LORD* (Isaiah 53:1). The miracles of Jesus showed Him to be God's Arm on earth. With a touch of His hand or a word from His mouth, the sick and dying were instantly made well.

> Great crowds came to him, bringing the lame, the blind, the crippled, the mute and many others, and laid them at his feet; and he healed them. (Matthew 15:30)

The words of the prophets were being fulfilled.

> The blind receive sight, the lame walk, those who have leprosy are cured, the deaf hear, the dead are raised, and the good news is preached to the poor. (Matthew 11:5 [Isaiah 35:4-6; 61:1])

There was no disease Jesus could not cure.

> Now a leper came to Him, imploring Him, kneeling down to Him and saying to Him, "If You are willing, You can make me clean."

> Then Jesus, moved with compassion, stretched out His hand and touched him, and said to him, "I am willing; be cleansed."

> As soon as He had spoken, immediately the leprosy left him, and he was cleansed. (Mark 1:40-42)

> When the sun was setting, the people brought to Jesus all who had various kinds of sickness, and laying his hands on each one, he healed them. Moreover, demons came out of many people, shouting, "You are the Son of God!"

> But he rebuked them and would not allow them to speak, because they knew he was the Christ. (Luke 4:40-41)

Jesus did not want the demons testifying about Him. These evil angels had witnessed His authority and power when He spoke the heavens and earth into place. They shuddered as they recalled the day He threw them out of heaven. And now He was living on earth as a man! Their master's dominion was crumbling. The King of glory had invaded their domain.

Wherever Jesus went, Satan's power was being weakened. Wherever Jesus went, sin's curse was being rolled back.

Along with the miracles, Jesus had a message:

> "The time has come," he said. "The kingdom of God has come near. Repent and believe the good news!" (Mark 1:15)

Scene 49

Dominion over Wind and Waves

Jesus selected twelve men to travel with Him and learn from Him. Also following Him were many women. They supported Jesus and His disciples by giving them food and money.

To those who believed in Him, Jesus' call was simple:

"Follow me." (Luke 5:27)

But His call was also costly:

"Anyone who loves his father or mother more than me is not worthy of me; anyone who loves his son or daughter more than me is not worthy of me." (Matthew 10:37)

Since several of His disciples were fishermen, Jesus often spent the day down by the Sea of Galilee. People came to Him from near and far.

Once again Jesus began teaching by the lakeshore. There was such a large crowd along the shore that he got into a boat and sat down and spoke from there. (Mark 4:1 NLT)

After a day of teaching, Jesus said to His disciples, "Let's go to the other side." He was already in the boat so they started out, leaving the crowd behind.

But soon a fierce storm came up. High waves were breaking into the boat, and it began to fill with water. Jesus was sleeping at the back of the boat with his head on a cushion. The disciples woke him up, shouting, "Teacher, don't you care that we're going to drown?"

When Jesus woke up, he rebuked the wind and said to the waves, "Silence! Be still!"

Suddenly the wind stopped, and there was a great calm.

Then he asked them, "Why are you afraid? Do you still have no faith?"

The disciples were absolutely terrified. "Who is this man?" they asked each other. "Even the wind and waves obey him!" (Mark 4:37-41 NLT)

Who is this man? A thousand years earlier, the prophet David had already answered the question:

They were at their wits' end. Then they cried out to the LORD in their trouble, and he brought them out of their distress. He stilled the storm to a whisper; the waves of the sea were hushed. (Psalm 107:27-29)

Who can calm the wind and waves by simply speaking to them?

The same Voice that created them.

SCENE 50
DOMINION OVER SIN

One day, four men carrying a stretcher with a crippled man came to the house where Jesus was.

The men tried to push their way inside but the room was so crowded they could not get in. So they climbed to the roof, removed some tiles, and lowered the mat into the room, right in front of Jesus.

> Seeing their faith, Jesus said to the paralyzed man,
> "My child, your sins are forgiven." (Mark 2:5 NLT)

Jesus knew that this man's greatest need was not to walk again, but to be forgiven of his sins.

> But some of the teachers of religious law who were
> sitting there thought to themselves, "What is he saying?
> This is blasphemy! Only God can forgive sins!"

> Jesus knew immediately what they were thinking, so he asked
> them, "Why do you question this in your hearts? Is it easier
> to say to the paralyzed man, 'Your sins are forgiven,' or 'Stand
> up, pick up your mat, and walk'? So I will prove to you that
> the Son of Man has the authority on earth to forgive sins."

> Then Jesus turned to the paralyzed man and said, "Stand up,
> pick up your mat, and go home!"

> And the man jumped up, grabbed his mat,
> and walked out through the stunned onlookers.

> They were all amazed and praised God, exclaiming,
> "We've never seen anything like this before!" (Mark 2:6-12 NLT)

The teachers of the law were blinded by their religion and pride. Their thoughts went something like this: *Jesus, you are a blasphemer! You are insulting God because you claim to forgive sins, but only God can do that!*

They were right in thinking that only God can forgive sins, but they were wrong in their conclusions about who Jesus is.

Who do *you* think Jesus is? Do you remember the meaning of His name? It means *The LORD Saves.*

In one Palestinian town where Jesus taught, the people came to this conclusion:

> "Now, we have heard for ourselves, and we know that
> this man really is the Savior of the world." (John 4:42)

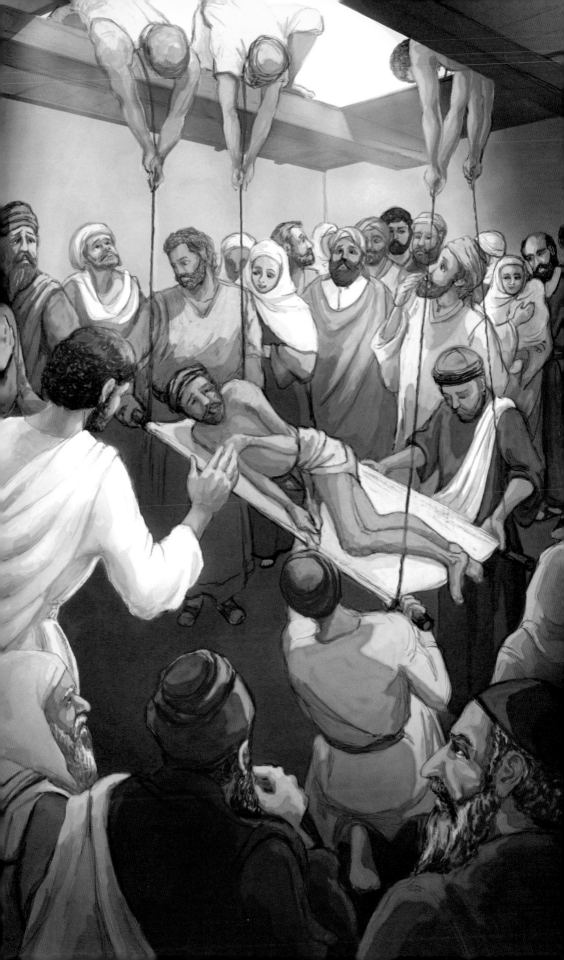

SCENE 51
DOMINION OVER DEATH

Jesus had dominion over every part of creation. Yet He didn't go around saying, "Worship Me! I am God! I am God!" He simply did the things that only God can do and then let people draw their own conclusions.

Based on the next two stories, who do you think Jesus is?

> Jesus went to a town called Nain, and his disciples and a large crowd went along with him. As he approached the town gate, a dead person was being carried out—the only son of his mother, and she was a widow. And a large crowd from the town was with her.

> When the Lord saw her, his heart went out to her and he said, "Don't cry."

> Then he went up and touched the coffin, and those carrying it stood still. He said, "Young man, I say to you, get up!"

> The dead man sat up and began to talk, and Jesus gave him back to his mother. They were all filled with awe and praised God. (Luke 7:12-16)

On another day, Jesus visited two grieving sisters, Martha and Mary. Four days earlier, their brother Lazarus had died.

> "Lord," Martha said to Jesus, "if you had been here, my brother would not have died…."

> Jesus said to her, "I am the resurrection and the life. He who believes in me will live, even though he dies; and whoever lives and believes in me will never die. Do you believe this?"

> "Yes, Lord," she told him, "I believe that you are the Christ, the Son of God, who was to come into the world."

> Jesus…came to the tomb. It was a cave with a stone laid across the entrance. "Take away the stone," he said.

> "But, Lord," said Martha, the sister of the dead man, "by this time there is a bad odor, for he has been there four days."

> Then Jesus said, "Did I not tell you that if you believed, you would see the glory of God?" So they took away the stone. Jesus called in a loud voice, "Lazarus, come out!" The dead man came out, his hands and feet wrapped with strips of linen. Jesus said to them, "Take off the grave clothes and let him go." (John 11:21,25-27,38-41,43-44)

The Lord Jesus is the only person in history who could say,

> "I AM the resurrection and the life."

His works proved that His words were true.

SCENE 52
THE PROVIDER

Huge crowds shadowed Jesus, sometimes for days at a time. Often they found Him in deserted areas, where He would go to spend time with His disciples. Sometimes the crowd got hungry.

This is what happened one afternoon as more than 5,000 people had gathered on a hillside east of the Sea of Galilee. So Jesus asked Philip, one of His disciples,

> "Where can we buy bread to feed all these people?" He was testing Philip, for he already knew what he was going to do.

> Philip replied, "It would take a small fortune to feed them!"

> Then Andrew, Simon Peter's brother, spoke up. "There's a young boy here with five barley loaves and two fish. But what good is that with this huge crowd?"

> "Tell everyone to sit down," Jesus ordered. So all of them—the men alone numbered five thousand—sat down on the grassy slopes.

> Then Jesus took the loaves, gave thanks to God, and passed them out to the people. Afterward he did the same with the fish. And they all ate until they were full.

> "Now gather the leftovers," Jesus told his disciples, "so that nothing is wasted."

> There were only five barley loaves to start with, but twelve baskets were filled with the pieces of bread the people did not eat! (John 6:5-13 NLT)

The next day some of the crowd came looking for Jesus. They wanted to make Him their king, but only so He could save them from their Roman oppressors and give them more food. Jesus told them,

> "You shouldn't be so concerned about perishable things like food. Spend your energy seeking the eternal life that I, the Son of Man,[19] can give you. For God the Father has sent me for that very purpose.

> "I am the bread of life. No one who comes to me will ever be hungry again. Those who believe in me will never thirst." (John 6:27,35 NLT)

Food can keep your body alive for a time, but only the Lord Jesus can give you true life, for time and for eternity.

Only Jesus can say,

> "I AM the bread of life."

SCENE 53
THE TEACHER

Jesus was not like the religious teachers who said things like, "Do this! Don't do that! Follow these rules! This is the way!" Only Jesus could say,

> "I AM the way and the truth and the life." (John 14:6)

Jesus was also different from the prophets who offered sacrifices for their sins and wrote about the coming Messiah. Jesus said,

> "Don't misunderstand why I have come. I did not come to abolish the law of Moses or the writings of the prophets. No, I came to fulfill them." (Matthew 5:17 NLT)

Jesus often taught His disciples how citizens of the kingdom of heaven should live in order to reflect the character and glory of their King.

> "You have heard that it was said, 'Love your neighbor and hate your enemy.' But I tell you: Love your enemies and pray for those who persecute you.

> "When you pray, do not be like the hypocrites, for they love to pray…to be seen by men. But when you pray, go into your room, close the door and pray to your Father, who is unseen. This, then, is how you should pray: 'Our Father in heaven, hallowed be your name, your kingdom come, your will be done on earth as it is in heaven. Give us today our daily bread….'

> "Do not worry, saying, 'What shall we eat?' or 'What shall we drink?' or 'What shall we wear?' For the pagans run after all these things, and your heavenly Father knows that you need them. But seek first his kingdom and his righteousness, and all these things will be given to you as well.

> "Watch out for false prophets. They come to you in sheep's clothing, but inwardly they are ferocious wolves.

> "Everyone who hears these words of mine and puts them into practice is like a wise man who built his house on the rock. The rain came down, the streams rose, and the winds blew and beat against that house; yet it did not fall, because it had its foundation on the rock.

> "But everyone who hears these words of mine and does not put them into practice is like a foolish man who built his house on sand. The rain came down, the streams rose, and the winds blew and beat against that house, and it fell with a great crash." (Matthew 5:43-44; 6:5-6,9-11,31-33; 7:15,24-27)

No one ever spoke like the Teacher from heaven.

SCENE 54

HIS MAJESTY

The teachers and priests of the Jews were not happy to see the crowds listening to Jesus. They wanted the people to listen to them, not Him!

One day the chief priests sent their temple guards to arrest Jesus, but they could not do it. When they returned, the priests asked them, "Why didn't you bring him in?" The guards answered,

> "No one ever spoke the way this man does." (John 7:46)

Not even the prophets spoke like Jesus. The prophets were like candles casting shimmering rays of light in a dark world, but the Messiah was "the sun of righteousness" (Malachi 4:2). Who needs candles once the sun has risen?

Jesus said,

> "I AM the light of the world. Whoever follows me will never walk in darkness, but will have the light of life." (John 8:12)

Jesus is the Word who in the beginning said, "Let there be light." He is the ultimate Source of physical and spiritual light.

As the time approached for the Messiah to fulfill His mission, He led three of His disciples, Peter, James, and John, up a high mountain.

> There he was transfigured before them. His face shone like the sun, and his clothes became as white as the light.

> Just then there appeared before them Moses and Elijah, talking with Jesus. … A bright cloud enveloped them, and a voice from the cloud said,

> "This is my Son, whom I love; with him I am well pleased. Listen to him!"

> When the disciples heard this, they fell face down to the ground, terrified. But Jesus came and touched them. "Get up," he said. "Don't be afraid."

> When they looked up, they saw no one except Jesus. (Matthew 17:1-3,5-8)

The disciples never forgot what they saw that day. Later, Peter would write, "We were eye-witnesses of his majesty!" (2 Peter 1:16) and John would say, "We have seen his glory, the glory of the One and Only, who came from the Father, full of grace and truth" (John 1:14).

But for now, the Son's glory would remain hidden in His body of flesh.

It was time for the King to fulfill His mission.

SCENE 55

HIS MISSION

For three years, the Lord Jesus had been traveling around Palestine "doing good, and healing all who were under the power of the devil" (Acts 10:38). The common people loved Him, but the religious leaders in Jerusalem were plotting to kill Him—and Jesus knew it.

> As the time approached for him to be taken up to heaven, Jesus resolutely set out for Jerusalem. (Luke 9:51)

If you knew that a band of evil men in a distant city were planning to capture, torture, and kill you, would you go there?

That is what Jesus did.

> From that time on Jesus began to explain to his disciples that he must go to Jerusalem and suffer many things at the hands of the elders, chief priests and teachers of the law, and that he must be killed and on the third day be raised to life. (Matthew 16:21)

This was not the sort of King the disciples were looking for. *A crucified Messiah? Surely God would not allow His Chosen One to suffer such pain and shame!* So Peter said to Jesus,

> "Never, Lord! This shall never happen to you!"

> Jesus turned and said to Peter, "Get behind me, Satan! You are a stumbling-block to me; you do not have in mind the things of God, but the things of men." (Matthew 16:22-23)

The disciples wanted a Messiah-King who would destroy the Roman occupiers and set up a new government in Jerusalem. Even as they journeyed, the disciples argued over who would get the top positions in the kingdom of God. So Jesus told His disciples,

> "Whoever wants to become great among you must be your servant… just as the Son of Man did not come to be served, but to serve, and to give his life as a ransom for many." (Matthew 20:26,28)

At His first coming to earth, the Messiah did not come to conquer political kingdoms and rule on earthly thrones; He came to conquer Satan and rule in human hearts. That is why Jesus taught,

> "The kingdom of God is within you." (Luke 17:21)

But before the King from heaven could reign in hearts (and later over the whole earth), the sin debt of the world had to be paid and death had to be defeated.

That was His mission.

The King Enters Jerusalem

Everything was going according to plan. As the Lord neared Jerusalem, He sent two disciples on an errand.

> "Go into that village over there," he told them. "As you enter it, you will see a young donkey tied there that no one has ever ridden. Untie it and bring it here. If anyone asks, 'Why are you untying that colt?' just say, 'The Lord needs it.'"
>
> So they went and found the colt, just as Jesus had said. And sure enough, as they were untying it, the owners asked them, "Why are you untying that colt?"
>
> And the disciples simply replied, "The Lord needs it." So they brought the colt to Jesus and threw their garments over it for him to ride on.
>
> As he rode along, the crowds spread out their garments on the road ahead of him. When he reached the place where the road started down the Mount of Olives, all of his followers began to shout and sing as they walked along, praising God for all the wonderful miracles they had seen. "Blessings on the King who comes in the name of the Lord! Peace in heaven, and glory in highest heaven!"
>
> But some of the Pharisees[20] among the crowd said, "Teacher, rebuke your followers for saying things like that!"
>
> He replied, "If they kept quiet, the stones along the road would burst into cheers!" (Luke 19:30-40 NLT)

What a different kind of king!

The Messiah-King did not storm the capital with a blast of trumpets and a mighty army. He did not enter on a gallant war-horse.

He rode in on a lowly donkey—a young donkey, an unbroken donkey (that would normally have kicked and bucked), an animal with the distinctive mark of a cross on its back and shoulders, and, most importantly, the only animal that could fulfill what the prophet Zechariah had written five hundred years earlier:

> Shout, Daughter of Jerusalem! See, your king comes to you, righteous and having salvation, gentle and riding on a donkey, on a colt, the foal of a donkey. (Zechariah 9:9)

Why did the Messiah-King not ride into Jerusalem on a mighty war-horse? Because He had not come to save the people from their Roman oppressors.

He had come to save His people from their sins.

SCENE 57
THE KING IS QUESTIONED

O ver the next few days, Jesus taught the people in the temple where, as a boy, He had amazed the scholars with His deep questions and wise answers. The leaders in the temple now had a different attitude:

"We don't want this man to be our king!" (Luke 19:14)

So they assaulted Jesus with explosive questions, hoping to turn the common people against Him.

Watching for their opportunity, the leaders sent spies pretending to be honest men. They tried to get Jesus to say something that could be reported to the Roman governor so he would arrest Jesus.

"Teacher," they said, "we know that you speak and teach what is right and are not influenced by what others think. You teach the way of God truthfully. Now tell us—is it right for us to pay taxes to Caesar or not?" (Luke 20:20-22 NLT)

What would Jesus answer? If He said, "Yes, pay taxes to the emperor," the Jewish population would accuse Him of disloyalty to their cause. On the other hand, if Jesus answered, "No, do not pay taxes," the Roman governor would hear of it and condemn Him for treason.

He saw through their trickery and said, "Show me a Roman coin. Whose picture and title are stamped on it?"

"Caesar's," they replied.

"Well then," he said, "give to Caesar what belongs to Caesar, and give to God what belongs to God."

So they failed to trap him by what he said in front of the people. Instead, they were amazed by his answer, and they became silent. (Luke 20:23-26 NLT)

Again and again, different groups of religious teachers tried to trap Jesus, but each time He answered them with perfect wisdom.

After that, no one dared to ask him any more questions.
(Matthew 22:46 NLT)

Put to shame, the men slipped away to conspire with the chief priests to have Jesus arrested and executed. What blindness! These priests, responsible to offer sacrifices on the temple altar, had no idea the Man they wanted to kill was the very One who was pictured in those sacrifices!

God's secret plan was about to be fulfilled.

SCENE 58

THE KING IS ARRESTED

It was the eve of the annual Feast of the Sacrifice, called the Passover.[16] The next day thousands of lambs would be killed.

Though Jesus knew that He too would be killed the next day, He spent the evening sharing a last supper with His disciples. During the meal, He took the bread, blessed it, broke it, and gave it to them to eat. He also passed around a cup. He told them the torn bread should make them think about His body and the red juice about His blood that would be shed to bring in the new covenant for the forgiveness of sins.

At midnight, He led His disciples to a garden called Gethsemane. There, knowing the horrors that awaited Him, He prayed to His Father.

Then, as if on cue, the religious leaders arrived with a mob of armed men. Jesus said to them,

> "Am I some dangerous revolutionary, that you come with swords and clubs to arrest me? Why didn't you arrest me in the Temple? I was there teaching every day. But this is all happening to fulfill the words of the prophets as recorded in the Scriptures."
>
> At that point, all the disciples deserted him and fled. (Matthew 26:55-56 NLT)

Jesus let the men bind Him and lead Him to the high priest's house where the Jewish rulers had gathered. There many men told lies about Jesus.

> Then the high priest stood up before them and asked Jesus, "Are you not going to answer? What is this testimony that these men are bringing against you?" But Jesus remained silent and gave no answer. Again the high priest asked him, "Are you the Christ, the Son of the Blessed One?"
>
> "I am," said Jesus. "And you will see the Son of Man sitting at the right hand of the Mighty One and coming on the clouds of heaven."
>
> The high priest tore his clothes. "Why do we need any more witnesses?" he asked. "You have heard the blasphemy. What do you think?"
>
> They all condemned him as worthy of death.
>
> Then some began to spit at him; they blindfolded him, struck him with his fists, and said, "Prophesy!" And the guards took him and beat him. (Mark 14:56,60-65)

The Jewish court had passed the death sentence, but it did not have the authority to carry it out. Only a Roman court could do that.

SCENE 59
THE KING IS CONDEMNED

It was early morning when the religious rulers and a growing mob led Jesus from the high priest's house through the streets of Jerusalem to the palace of the Roman governor, Pontius Pilate.

The religious leaders wanted Pilate to put Jesus to death.

> They began at once to state their case: "This man has been leading our people to ruin by telling them not to pay their taxes to the Roman government and by claiming he is the Messiah, a king."

> [After interrogating Jesus] Pilate turned to the leading priests and to the crowd and said, "I find nothing wrong with this man!"
> (Luke 23:2,4 NLT)

> "If he were not a criminal," they replied, "we would not have handed him over to you." …

> Pilate then went back inside the palace, summoned Jesus and asked him, "Are you the king of the Jews? … What is it you have done?"

> Jesus said, "My kingdom is not of this world. If it were, my servants would fight to prevent my arrest by the Jews. But now my kingdom is from another place."

> "You are a king, then!" said Pilate.

> Jesus answered, "You are right in saying I am a king. In fact, for this reason I was born, and for this I came into the world, to testify to the truth. Everyone on the side of truth listens to me."

> "What is truth?" Pilate asked.

> With this he went out again to the Jews and said, "I find no basis for a charge against him." (John 18:30,33,35-38)

But the mob kept screaming,

> "Crucify him! Crucify him!"

> For the third time he spoke to them: "Why? What crime has this man committed? I have found in him no grounds for the death penalty. Therefore I will have him punished and then release him."

> But with loud shouts they insistently demanded that he be crucified, and their shouts prevailed. (Luke 23:21-23)

Pilate knew Jesus was innocent, but because he was afraid of the religious leaders and their mob, he condemned Jesus to death.

Scene 60
The King is Crowned

Pilate sentenced Jesus to the extreme penalty of Roman law: a brutal beating followed by crucifixion. Condemned victims were flogged with whips imbedded with sharp pieces of metal.

Seven hundred years earlier, the Lord had told the prophet Isaiah to write:

> "I offered my back to those who beat me, my cheeks to those who pulled out my beard; I did not hide my face from mocking and spitting." (Isaiah 50:6)

The gospel tells us what happened after the Lord was whipped.

> Some of the governor's soldiers took Jesus into their headquarters and called out the entire battalion.
>
> They stripped him and put a scarlet robe on him.
>
> They made a crown of long, sharp thorns and put it on his head, and they placed a stick in his right hand as a scepter. Then they knelt before him in mockery, yelling, "Hail! King of the Jews!" And they spit on him and grabbed the stick and beat him on the head with it. (Matthew 27:27-30 NLT)

The soldiers were ignorant of the meaning of the crown of thorns they had jammed onto Jesus' head. Thorns were part of the curse that came over the earth because of Adam's sin. The holy King of glory had come to take sin's curse for us.

> When they were finally tired of mocking him, they took off the robe and put his own clothes on him again. Then they led him away to be crucified. (Matthew 27:31 NLT)

Two convicted criminals were also led out with Jesus. Each was made to carry his own cross to the place of execution.

Partway into the grim parade, the Roman soldiers forced a man from north Africa to carry Jesus' cross for Him. Then on they went, through Jerusalem's crowded streets, outside the city walls, and up a hill called Golgotha, the northern part of Mount Moriah where, about 1,900 years earlier, the prophet Abraham had said,

> "God himself will provide the lamb for the burnt offering, my son." (Genesis 22:8).

It was time for that Lamb to die.

SCENE 61

THE KING IS CRUCIFIED

Crucifixion is the most horrific state-sponsored method of execution ever devised. To add public shame to excruciating pain, the Roman soldiers stripped victims naked before driving nails through their hands and feet, into a cross or tree.

> When they came to the place called the Skull, there they crucified him, along with the criminals—one on his right, the other on his left. Jesus said, "Father, forgive them, for they do not know what they are doing."
>
> And they divided up his clothes by casting lots. The people stood watching, and the rulers even sneered at him. They said, "He saved others; let him save himself if he is the Christ of God, the Chosen One." (Luke 23:33-35)

If Jesus had saved Himself, He could not have saved us. The crowd had no idea they were fulfilling what the Lord had spoken to the prophet David:

> "They have pierced my hands and my feet. … People stare and gloat over me. They divide my garments among them and cast lots for my clothing. … All who see me mock me; they hurl insults, shaking their heads: '… Let the LORD rescue him. Let him deliver him, since he delights in him!'" (Psalm 22:16-18,6-8)

God's rescue plan was being fulfilled in every detail.

On the same mountain[11] where the prophet Abraham had said, "God himself will provide the lamb," and "The LORD Will Provide" (Genesis 22:8,14), God had provided His very own Lamb—Jesus.

Do you remember how the innocent ram was sacrificed on the wood on an altar to ransom Abraham's condemned son? Now the sinless Son of God was being sacrificed on a wooden cross to ransom Adam's condemned descendants. God spared Abraham's son, but He "did not spare his own Son, but gave him up for us all" (Romans 8:32).

> For God so loved the world that He gave His only begotten Son, that whoever believes in Him should not perish but have everlasting life. (John 3:16 NKJV)
>
> God paid a ransom to save you from the empty life you inherited from your ancestors. And the ransom he paid was not mere gold or silver. He paid for you with the precious lifeblood of Christ, the sinless, spotless Lamb of God. (1 Peter 1:18-19 NLT)

That is how much you are worth to God.

SCENE 62
THE SAVIOR-KING

To fulfill God's rescue plan, the Lord Jesus felt the shame sin brings. He was cursed in our place. He took the punishment we deserve.

On the day Adam broke God's law, God made it known that the Messiah would one day crush the Serpent. God had told Satan,

> "He will crush your head, and you will strike his heel." (Genesis 3:15)

This ancient, mysterious prophecy about Satan striking the Savior's heel foretold the shame and pain the Lamb of God would suffer on the cross as "he was pierced for our transgressions" (Isaiah 53:5).

Those who crucified Jesus were ignorant of God's secret plan.

> None of the rulers of this age understood it, for if they had, they would not have crucified the Lord of glory.

> For the message of the cross is foolishness to those who are perishing, but to us who are being saved it is the power of God. (1 Corinthians 2:8; 1:18)

Jesus' cross was placed between the two criminals.

> One of the criminals who hung there hurled insults at him: "Aren't you the Christ? Save yourself and us!"

> But the other criminal rebuked him. "Don't you fear God," he said, "since you are under the same sentence? We are punished justly, for we are getting what our deeds deserve. But this man has done nothing wrong." Then he said, "Jesus, remember me when you come into your kingdom."

> Jesus answered him, "I tell you the truth, today you will be with me in paradise." (Luke 23:39-43)

The first criminal only wanted to be saved from his physical sufferings. He didn't think he needed a Savior to die in his place.

The second criminal had also insulted Jesus. But as he faced death, he had a change of heart. He wanted the Lord to rescue him from Satan's kingdom. He wanted to become a citizen of God's kingdom, if the King would have him. Jesus' answer left no doubt:

> "Today you will be with me in paradise." (Luke 23:43)

Later that evening, both criminals died. One went to hell. The other went to paradise. What made the difference?

One did not put his trust in the Savior-King. The other did.

SCENE 63
THE FINAL SACRIFICE

It is noon. Jesus has already been on the cross for three hours. Dark clouds roll in. Day becomes like night. Terrified onlookers scatter. An eerie silence covers the hill. Three hours later, Jesus cries out,

"My God, my God, why have you forsaken me?" (Matthew 27:46)

On the altar of the cross, the eternal Son of God felt the horror of being separated from God in heaven. During those hours of darkness, hidden from the eyes of men, God took all our sins and put them on His holy Son. Jesus became the final sin offering.

As the past, present, and future sins of the world were loaded onto Jesus, God in heaven had to look away because His "eyes are too pure to look on evil" (Habakkuk 1:13). For three long hours, God's anger against sin blazed down on His own burnt offering. Like a lamb sacrificed on an altar, the Lamb of God was suspended on the cross between heaven and earth, between God and man. The infinite One endured our hell in time so that we need not endure it in eternity.

Then it was done.

Knowing that He had absorbed the punishment sinners deserve and that He had fulfilled the prophecies of the Old Testament, Jesus said,

"It is finished!"

Then he bowed his head and released his spirit. (John 19:30 NLT)

At that moment the curtain of the temple was torn in two from top to bottom. The earth shook and the rocks split. (Matthew 27:51)

For centuries, lambs had been killed and burned on the temple altar. When Jesus died, God tore open the curtain that hid the special room where the blood was sprinkled each year to cover sin. By ripping the curtain, God was declaring: *It is finished! The sin debt is paid in full! My Lamb has shed His holy blood for the sin of the world. I will no longer accept animal blood for sins. My beloved Son is the Final Sacrifice. For all who believe in Him, heaven's door is wide open!* (See the book of Hebrews in the New Testament.)

Seven hundred years earlier, the prophet Isaiah wrote,

He was pierced for our rebellion, crushed for our sins. He was beaten so we could be whole. He was whipped so we could be healed. All of us, like sheep, have strayed away. We have left God's paths to follow our own. Yet the LORD laid on him the sins of us all. (Isaiah 53:5-6 NLT)

It is finished.

SCENE 64
THE KING IS BURIED

Jesus of Nazareth was dead. Just to be sure, a soldier rammed a spear into His side. Blood and water gushed out.

The disciples' hopes were also dead. Thinking Jesus should have crushed the Romans and set up His kingdom on earth, the disciples had not yet understood His promise to rise on the third day.

The dead bodies of crucified victims were usually tossed onto a garbage dump outside the city or into a mass grave. Not so with Jesus' body. Seven hundred years earlier, the prophet Isaiah had written,

> "He was assigned a grave with the wicked, and
> with the rich in his death…." (Isaiah 53:9)

God planned for His Son to be buried in a tomb of honor.

> As evening approached, there came a rich man from Arimathea, named Joseph, who had himself become a disciple of Jesus. Going to Pilate, he asked for Jesus' body, and Pilate ordered that it be given to him. (Matthew 27:57-58)

Before Jesus' death, Joseph of Arimathea and his friend Nicodemus had been secret followers of Jesus the Messiah. They were afraid of the religious leaders. But after seeing Jesus suffer on the cross, they weren't afraid anymore. So they took the body of Jesus, washed it, and wrapped it in strips of clean linen along with about 35 kilos of myrrh, the same kind of costly embalming spice the Magi had given the child Jesus. Next they placed the body in Joseph's own new tomb. After rolling a huge stone across the entrance, they went home.

It was a royal burial, fit for a king.

The next morning the religious leaders went to Pilate.

> "Sir," they said, "we remember that while he was still alive that deceiver said, 'After three days I will rise again.' So give the order for the tomb to be made secure until the third day. Otherwise, his disciples may come and steal the body and tell the people that he has been raised from the dead. This last deception will be worse than the first."

> "Take a guard," Pilate answered. "Go, make the tomb as secure as you know how." So they went and made the tomb secure by putting a seal on the stone and posting the guard. (Matthew 27:63-66)

Meanwhile, inside the grave, what was happening to Jesus' body?

Nothing.

SCENE 65
THE EMPTY TOMB

Since the day Adam sinned, Death had reigned like a cruel king over the human family. If Jesus had ever sinned, Death would also have made His body begin to decay, stink, and slowly turn into dust. But 1,000 years earlier, the prophet David had written,

> "You will not…let your Holy One see decay." (Psalm 16:9-10)

Death and the grave had no power over the One who never sinned.

On the third day after Jesus was killed and buried, early Sunday morning, several women came to the tomb to pay their respects. Suddenly, there was a great earthquake as an angel came down from heaven, pushed aside the stone, and sat on it. The soldiers fainted, but the angel told the women,

> "Don't be afraid!" he said. "I know you are looking for Jesus, who was crucified. He isn't here! He has been raised from the dead, just as he said would happen. Come, see where his body was lying. And now, go quickly and tell his disciples he has been raised from the dead…."
>
> The women ran quickly from the tomb. They were very frightened but also filled with great joy, and they rushed to find the disciples to give them the angel's message.
>
> And as they went, Jesus met them. "Greetings!" he said. And they ran to him, held his feet, and worshiped him. (Matthew 28:5-9 NLT)

Meanwhile, the soldiers came into the city and told the religious leaders what had happened. So the leaders bribed them with a huge sum of money, telling them,

> "You must say, 'Jesus' disciples came during the night while we were sleeping, and they stole his body.'" (Matthew 28:13 NLT)

But their lies could not hide the truth. *The Tomb was empty!*

By His death, Jesus paid our sin debt.
By His burial, Jesus went down into the pit of death and decay.
By His resurrection, Jesus overcame Death, and now says,

> "Don't be afraid! I am the First and the Last. I am the living one who died. Look, I am alive forever and ever! And I hold the keys of death and the grave." (Revelation 1:17-18 NLT)

For all who believe this good news, Death is merely the door that opens into the presence of the King who says,

> "Because I live, you also will live." (John 14:19)

The Message of the Prophets

O n the day of His resurrection, Jesus appeared to many of His disciples: first to the women, then to Peter, and next to two travelers…

That same day two of Jesus' followers were walking to the village of Emmaus, seven miles from Jerusalem.

Jesus himself suddenly came and began walking with them. But God kept them from recognizing him. He asked them, "What are you discussing so intently as you walk along?"

They stopped short, sadness written across their faces. Then one of them, Cleopas, replied, "You must be the only person in Jerusalem who hasn't heard about all the things that have happened there the last few days."

"What things?" Jesus asked. (Luke 24:13,15-19 NLT)

The travelers told how they had hoped Jesus of Nazareth would have been the Messiah to conquer their enemies. But He was crucified! And now the tomb was empty. *It made no sense!*

Then Jesus said to them, "You foolish people! You find it so hard to believe all that the prophets wrote in the Scriptures. Wasn't it clearly predicted that the Messiah would have to suffer all these things before entering his glory?"

Then Jesus took them through the writings of Moses and all the prophets, explaining from all the Scriptures the things concerning himself.

By this time they were nearing Emmaus and the end of their journey. Jesus acted as if he were going on, but they begged him, "Stay the night with us, since it is getting late." So he went home with them.

As they sat down to eat, he took the bread and blessed it. Then he broke it and gave it to them. Suddenly, their eyes were opened, and they recognized him. And at that moment he disappeared!

They said to each other, "Didn't our hearts burn within us as he talked with us on the road and explained the Scriptures to us?" (Luke 24:25-32 NLT)

They jumped up and hurried back to Jerusalem to tell the disciples:
The Lord is alive! He is the Savior promised in the Scriptures!
He is the Lamb pictured in the sacrifices! He is the LORD!

At last the message of the prophets made sense.

Perfect sense.

SCENE 67

A TRANSFORMED BODY

It was Sunday evening. The disciples were together, with the doors locked. Suddenly Jesus appeared in the room and said,

"Peace be with you!"

After he said this, he showed them his hands and side. The disciples were overjoyed when they saw the Lord. (John 20:19-20)

Thomas, one of Jesus' twelve disciples, was not there that evening. Later, the disciples told him, "We have seen the Lord!"

But Thomas said to them, "Unless I see the nail marks in his hands and put my finger where the nails were, and put my hand into his side, I will not believe it."

A week later his disciples were in the house again, and Thomas was with them. Though the doors were locked, Jesus came and stood among them and said, "Peace be with you!"

Then he said to Thomas, "Put your finger here; see my hands. Reach out your hand and put it into my side. Stop doubting and believe."

Thomas said to him, "My Lord and my God!"

Then Jesus told him, "Because you have seen me, you have believed; blessed are those who have not seen and yet have believed." (John 20:24-29)

Over the next forty days, the Lord would abruptly appear to His followers, talk with them, and then disappear. Jesus' resurrected body could go through walls and travel at the speed of thought. While He is the first to have such a body, He will not be the last.

Just as we have borne the image of the earthly man, so shall we bear the image of the heavenly man.

For since death came through a man, the resurrection of the dead comes also through a man. For as in Adam all die, so in Christ all will be made alive. (1 Corinthians 15:49,21-22)

Do you understand that you are a helpless sinner with no way to earn the right to live in God's kingdom? Do you believe the Lord Jesus Christ died in *your* place, for *your* sins and came back to life, defeating death for *you*? If so, then God says you are no longer *in Adam*. God sees you as righteous *in Christ*. One day you too will receive a transformed body—just like His.

But without the nail scars.

SCENE 68
THE DEPARTURE

The dominion Adam had lost to Satan, Jesus had taken back. By His total authority over the devil and demons, wind and waves, sickness and hunger, sin and death—Jesus showed He was in perfect control. Even when the religious leaders and soldiers arrested, tortured, and crucified Him, He had let them do it.

That is why, before going back up to His Father's home, the Lord Jesus said to His disciples:

> "All authority in heaven and on earth has been given to me. Therefore go and make disciples of all nations, baptizing[21] them in the name of the Father and of the Son and of the Holy Spirit, and teaching them to obey everything I have commanded you. And surely I am with you always, to the very end of the age." (Matthew 28:18-20)

Jesus also told His followers,

> "A new command I give you: Love one another. As I have loved you, so you must love one another. By this all men will know that you are my disciples, if you love one another." (John 13:34-35)

Forty days after His resurrection, Jesus gathered His disciples on the Mount of Olives outside Jerusalem. The disciples wanted to know when He would return.

Jesus answered,

> "It is not for you to know the times or dates the Father has set by his own authority. But you will receive power when the Holy Spirit[22] comes on you; and you will be my witnesses in Jerusalem, and in all Judea and Samaria, and to the ends of the earth."

> After he said this, he was taken up before their very eyes, and a cloud hid him from their sight. They were looking intently up into the sky as he was going, when suddenly two men dressed in white stood beside them.

> "Men of Galilee," they said, "why do you stand here looking into the sky? This same Jesus, who has been taken from you into heaven, will come back in the same way you have seen him go into heaven."

> Then they returned to Jerusalem.... (Acts 1:7-12)

Meanwhile up in heaven, it was time for the King to be "crowned with glory and honor" (Psalm 8:5; Hebrews 2:9).

Scene 69
The Victory Celebration

I magine the splendor. The colors. The music. The excitement. A hundred million angels talking among themselves: *The King is coming home! But He will look different. The One who created man in the image of God will forevermore bear the image of man!*

A hush settles over the celestial city.

Suddenly the silence is broken with a majestic chorus of trumpets, followed by a booming proclamation:

> Open up, ancient gates! Open up, ancient doors,
> And let the King of glory enter.
>   Who is the King of glory?
> The LORD, strong and mighty, the LORD, invincible in battle!
>   Who is the King of glory?
> The LORD Almighty—he is the King of glory! (Psalm 24:7-8,10 NLT)

The gates swing open wide and, to the thunderous applause of heaven, in comes the Champion, the Lamb, the battle-scarred Son of Man—*Jesus!* Through the adoring multitude He walks, up to His Father's throne. Turning, He looks out over Adam's ransomed race, and sits down.

Mission accomplished.

Later, heaven's citizens sing this new song to their beloved King:

> "You are worthy…for you were killed, and your blood has ransomed people for God from every tribe and language and people and nation." (Revelation 5:9 NLT)

Then the angels encircle the throne, praising God, and saying,

> "Worthy is the Lamb, who was slain, to receive…honor and glory and praise!" (Revelation 5:12)

On earth today, most of Adam's descendants are still captives in Satan's doomed kingdom of sin and death. But freedom is available. By His death, burial, and resurrection, the Lord Jesus won the decisive battle. To all who trust Him, He says,

> "Don't let your hearts be troubled. Trust in God, and trust also in me. There is more than enough room in my Father's home. …When everything is ready, I will come and get you, so that you will always be with me where I am."

> "I am the way, the truth, and the life. No one can come to the Father except through me." (John 14:1-3,6 NLT)

SCENE 70
THE KING IS COMING BACK

One of these days, while the world is busy with its trivial pursuits and false religions, the King of glory will return to Earth, but not on a lowly donkey, nor to be mocked and crowned with thorns.

The risen King gave John a preview of that future day:

> I saw heaven standing open and there before me was a white horse, whose rider is called Faithful and True. With justice he judges and makes war. His eyes are like blazing fire, and on his head are many crowns. … His name is the Word of God. The armies of heaven were following him, riding on white horses and dressed in fine linen, white and clean…. On his robe and on his thigh he has this name written: KING OF KINGS AND LORD OF LORDS. (Revelation 19:11-14,16)

As the King returns, a voice will thunder from heaven:

> "The kingdom of the world has become the kingdom of our Lord and of his Christ, and he will reign for ever and ever!" (Revelation 11:15)

The King's enemies will melt before Him. He will then bind Satan and show a weary world what a righteous government looks like. It will be Earth's finest hour.

> The LORD will be king over the whole earth. On that day there will be one LORD, and his name the only name. (Prophet Zechariah 14:9)

On the Day of Judgment, the LORD Jesus will be the Judge.

> He sat on a fiery throne with wheels of blazing fire, and a river of fire was pouring out, flowing from his presence. Millions of angels ministered to him; many millions stood to attend him. Then the court began its session, and the books were opened. (Prophet Daniel 7:9-10 NLT)

Satan and his kingdom of darkness will be "thrown into the lake of burning sulphur" (Revelation 20:10). At last, the Serpent's head will be forever crushed.

As for the citizens of the kingdom of light, God will make for them "a new heaven and a new earth. … They will be his people, and God himself will be with them and be their God. He will wipe every tear from their eyes. There will be no more death or mourning or crying" (Revelation 21:1,3-4).

At last, the prayer of all who love their King will be forever realized:

> "Your kingdom come, your will be done on earth as it is in heaven!"
> (Matthew 6:10)

Is this your prayer? Have you bowed to the King of glory?

Is He *your* King?

Closing

I tell you the truth, whoever hears my
word and believes him who sent me has
eternal life and will not be condemned;
he has crossed over from death to life.

— Jesus, King of Glory (John 5:24)

He was in the world, and though the world
was made through him, the world did not
recognize him. … Yet to all who received
him, to those who believed in his name, he
gave the right to become children of God.

— the Gospel (John 1:10,12)

HAPPILY EVER AFTER?

People of all ages love imaginary tales of romance and rescue, stories with happy endings. People tell such tales because the one true God has built into the human heart a yearning to be delivered from evil and to live happily ever after. But the story of the King of glory is no imaginary tale.

A make-believe story is not written by forty prophets over fifteen centuries, but God's book is. Fiction is not confirmed by hundreds of prophecies and archaeological discoveries, but God's story is.

A make-believe superhero is not the dividing point of history, but Jesus is. Fantasy cannot remove our sin and shame, bring us to God, and give us a new heart filled with His love, joy, and peace, but Jesus can.

By fulfilling the Scriptures of the prophets, Jesus the Messiah has made it possible for Adam's descendants to live forever with their Creator-King. But not all will live in His kingdom.

Just as God made His one rule clear to Adam about living in the earthly garden, so God has made His one rule clear to Adam's descendants about living in the heavenly city:

> Nothing impure will ever enter it, nor will anyone who does what is shameful or deceitful, but only those whose names are written in the Lamb's book of life. (Revelation 21:27)

The Lamb's book of life is the heavenly registry with the name of every person who, since the time of Adam, has trusted God's way of salvation. The King of glory will not force you or your family to believe in Him and what He has done to rescue you from Satan, sin, death, and hell.

There will be no unwilling subjects in His kingdom. But because the King does not want anyone to perish, He closes His book with an invitation, a warning, and a promise:

> "Whoever is thirsty, let him come; and whoever wishes, let him take the free gift of the water of life. I warn everyone who hears the words of the prophecy of this book: If anyone adds anything to them, God will add to him the plagues described in this book…. He who testifies to these things says, 'Yes, I am coming soon.'"

> "Amen! Come, Lord Jesus!" (Revelation 22:17-20)

After Adam sinned, what did he say to God when God came into the garden calling out to him? Adam shamefully answered,

"I heard you in the garden, and I was afraid." (Genesis 3:10)

But now, how do some of Adam's descendants react to the Lord's promise to come to earth for them? They joyfully answer,

"Amen! Come, Lord Jesus!" (Revelation 22:20)

What brought about such transformation? Why are some people no longer afraid to stand before the Judge of the earth? Why are they so excited about seeing the King face to face?

It is because they believe His story and message.

The prophet Isaiah wrote,

Who has believed our message? … All of us, like sheep, have strayed away. We have left God's paths to follow our own. Yet the LORD laid on him the sins of us all. (Isaiah 53:1,6 NLT)

Isaiah summed up the King's story and message in three statements:

1. We have a problem.

"We have left God's paths to follow our own."

2. God has the solution.

"The LORD laid on [His Son] the sins of us all."

3. We have a choice.

"Who has believed our message?"

Do you believe the King?

We accept man's testimony, but God's testimony is greater because it is the testimony of God, which he has given about his Son. …

Anyone who does not believe God has made him out to be a liar, because he has not believed the testimony God has given about his Son. And this is the testimony: God has given us eternal life, and this life is in his Son. He who has the Son has life; he who does not have the Son of God does not have life.

I write these things to you who believe in the name of the Son of God so that you may know that you have eternal life. (1 John 5:9-13)

Yes, you can *know*. The King does not keep you guessing.

Have you turned your back on man's religion and believed God's testimony? If so, then you will spend eternity with the King…

… happily ever after.

THE BAD NEWS

As we read at the beginning of His book, the King of the universe created man in His own image and likeness. He made humans for His glory. People would be His special treasure, close friends, and holy citizens in His kingdom of light. But first there must be a time of testing.

The LORD God gave Adam a small test with big consequences. God told him that he was free to eat from all the trees of the garden except one. What did God say would happen to Adam if he broke this one rule?

 Did God tell Adam that he must begin to recite prayers, fast, and do enough good deeds to balance out his bad deeds? *No!* God said, "When you eat of it *you will surely die*" (Genesis 2:17).

We know what happened. Man chose to disobey his Creator-King. Adam and Eve sinned. But did they drop dead that same day? No. So what did God mean when He said, "When you eat of it you will surely die"?

What, according to the Scriptures, is the meaning of death?

 Look at the picture. What is happening with the branch? What will happen to it after it is broken from the tree? Will it be alive? Or dead?

The branch might still look alive, but it will be dead because it has been separated from its source of life.

Death means *separation*. This is bad news.

When Adam and Eve chose to go their own way instead of God's way they lost their connection with God, like a branch cut off the tree. Their relationship with God was dead. They no longer wanted to be with Him. They tried to hide. Adam and Eve were dead spiritually.

> Your sins have cut you off from God. Because of your sin, he has turned away and will not listen anymore. (Isaiah 59:2 NLT)

 Adam and Eve also began to die physically. Even as the leaves on a broken branch do not dry up instantly, so their bodies did not return to dust the day they sinned. But the aging process had begun. Death was an enemy from which they would not escape.

But the bad news gets worse. Unless God provided rescue, Adam and Eve faced eternal separation from God in "the eternal fire prepared for the devil and his angels" (Matthew 25:41).

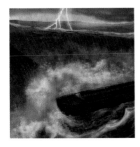

Some people mock the idea of hell—a lake of fire where souls contaminated by sin will be quarantined for all eternity. But is it wise to mock what we do not understand? As humans, we cannot grasp the concept of eternity. It is another dimension.[8] People also mocked the prophet Noah as he built the ark and warned them of the coming flood, but once the door of the ark was closed and the flood came, they understood the truth they had mocked. In a similar way, the moment people enter hell, they will understand its solemn logic.

They will be punished with everlasting destruction and shut out from the presence of the Lord and from the majesty of his power. (2 Thessalonians 1:9)

The King will not allow sin to pollute His universe forever.

Sin is the most destructive force and far-reaching disaster on our planet. Sin is the cause of all evil.

 Like a contagious disease, Adam's sin has infected us all. Just as each twig and leaf on a broken branch is dead, so each of us is affected by Adam's sin. We are all a part of the Adam branch.

When Adam sinned, sin entered the world. Adam's sin brought death, so death spread to everyone, for everyone sinned. (Romans 5:12 NLT)

 Back in Moses' day, people had the same wrong idea that people have today. They hoped that if they did more good than bad, God would show them mercy on the Day of Judgment. To correct their wrong thinking, God came down on Mount Sinai in blazing fire and gave the people ten commands to obey. Anyone who did not keep all ten rules perfectly was declared guilty and worthy of death.

 The Ten Commandments are like a mirror. If your face is dirty, a mirror helps you see the dirt, but it cannot remove the dirt. In a similar way, the Commandments were not given to make us right with God. Instead, they show us that we are guilty sinners before a holy God. We are unfit to live in His righteous kingdom. We are helpless sinners in need of a perfect Savior.

For everyone has sinned; we all fall short of God's glorious standard. (Romans 3:23 NLT)

The bad news is that we do not measure up to God's perfect standard of goodness. The good news is that there is one person in history who did.

His name is Jesus.

THE GOOD NEWS

The LORD is perfect in justice and mercy. Justice means that the full penalty of the law has been carried out against my sin. Mercy means that the penalty of the law has not been carried out against me.

How could God punish our sin without punishing us?

The answer is found in the Lord Jesus Christ, who came to our rescue.

 In Old Testament times, before Jesus came, God set up *the law of the sin offering* to rescue sinners from *the law of sin and death*. God accepted the blood of innocent animals as a payment for sin. This is how He punished sin without punishing the sinner.

But is a lamb a fair trade for a man? No. Animal blood could only picture what justice really required.

What kind of blood could pay off the sin debt of the world? Only the blood of a perfect, infinite Man. The Creator-Word Himself became that Man.

 "In the beginning was the Word … The Word became flesh and made his dwelling among us. We have seen his glory, the glory of the One and Only, who came from the Father, full of grace and truth." (John 1:1,14)

 The blood of lambs could only *cover* sin. Jesus is "the Lamb of God, who *takes away* the sin of the world!" (John 1:29)

 Remember Abel? God put Abel's sins on the lamb. The lamb was Abel's temporary sin-bearer. Jesus is our permanent Sin-Bearer. God loaded all our sins onto Him.

 The lamb that was killed and burned to ashes in Abel's place was a picture of Jesus who paid the full penalty for our sins. That is why, just before He died, Jesus shouted in victory, "It is finished!" (John 19:30)

Justice is satisfied. Mercy is available.

It is this Good News that saves you if you firmly believe it …
Christ died for our sins, just as the Scriptures said. He was buried, and he was raised from the dead on the third day, as the Scriptures said.
(1 Corinthians 15:2-4 NLT)

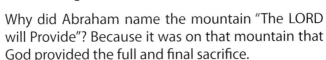

T hink of Abraham and his son. Why did God send them to a specific distant mountain for the sacrifice?

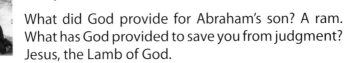

God was marking out the place where His own Son would go to die for the sins of the world.

Why did Abraham name the mountain "The LORD will Provide"? Because it was on that mountain that God provided the full and final sacrifice.

What did God provide for Abraham's son? A ram. What has God provided to save you from judgment? Jesus, the Lamb of God.

Do you fear death and judgment? If you put your total trust in Jesus as your Savior you need not fear, because God has received full payment from Him for your sins and raised Him back to life.

Now think back to Adam and Eve. Their sin and shame made them cover up with fig leaves and want to hide from God. In His justice and mercy, God exposed their sin and clothed them in the skins of sacrificed animals. The shed blood of the animals pictured what was necessary to cover their sin, and the skins of the animals pictured what was necessary to cover their shame.

We all share our ancestors' sin and shame. We fall short of God's righteousness. We are unfit to live with Him. The good news is that on the cross Jesus Christ took our sin and shame. During those hours of darkness, He experienced the separation from God that we deserve. And then He died. But since He had no sin of His own, the tomb could not hold Him.

Because of Jesus' death and resurrection, God offers to cleanse and clothe you: to exchange your sins for His righteousness.

We are all infected and impure with sin. When we display our righteous deeds, they are nothing but filthy rags. (Isaiah 64:6 NLT)

I am overwhelmed with joy in the LORD my God! For he has dressed me with the clothing of salvation and draped me in a robe of righteousness. (Isaiah 61:10 NLT)

God made him who had no sin to be sin for us, so that in him we might become the righteousness of God. (2 Corinthians 5:21)

On Judgment Day, will you stand before God in the rags of your own religious efforts?

Or will you stand robed in the pure righteousness of Christ?

YOUR RESPONSE TO THE KING

Imagine yourself walking through a lonely forest. Which would you rather meet—a lamb or a lion?

At His first coming, the King of glory was called *The Lamb*. He came in humility to save sinners. When the King returns, He will be called *The Lion*. He will come in majesty to judge unrepentant sinners.

When Jesus comes back, will you rejoice in the presence of your Savior-King or will you tremble before your Judge-King? It all depends on your response to God's message.

When Jesus began to travel and teach, some of His first words were,

"Repent and believe the good news!" (Mark 1:15)

"Repent" means to *change your mind* about what you are trusting in for the right to live in God's kingdom. It means to stop trusting your own way and to start trusting and following God's way.

"Believe the good news" means to *put your faith in the Savior* who died for your sins and rose again to give you new life. But what does it mean to put your faith in someone?

Let me illustrate with a first-hand story from West Africa. It's about two women, Fatu and Bintu.

Both had infections in their eyes. Fatu went to the hospital. The doctor gave her antibiotic eye drops. Her eyes were cured. Bintu went to the traditional healer. He rubbed his "cure" into her eyes. Her eyes turned white and she became blind.

Both Fatu and Bintu had faith. Both women acted on their faith by going to a healer they trusted—but how different the outcome.

When it comes to eternity, everyone trusts in something or someone. Many hang their hope on the religion of their parents. Some side with those who say that life ends at the grave. Others come up with their own ideas about life, death, and eternity. In the end, only one question will matter: Did you choose the truth?

As for me, I've made my choice. I trust the King, who said,

"Everyone on the side of truth listens to me." (John 18:37)

He is the One I want to live with forever. He's the One "who loved me and gave himself for me" (Galatians 2:20).

He is not just *a* king. He's *my* King!

The first man was made to reflect God's image. That image was spoiled by sin. Jesus Christ, "the image of the invisible God" (Colossians 1:15), came to give you new life and to restore God's image in you.

If you have put your faith in Jesus Christ the King of glory, then, in the eyes of God, you are no longer *in Adam*. You are *in Christ*. You are a favored citizen of heaven and a beloved child of God. You are God's own treasure, which He ransomed with the blood of His own Son.

As a newborn member of God's family you can now call God *Father*. But with great privilege comes great responsibility.

> As obedient children, do not conform to the evil desires you had when you lived in ignorance. But just as he who called you is holy, so be holy in all you do. (1 Peter 1:14-15)

As a follower of Christ, you are called to forgive, love, and pray for all people, even your enemies. Jesus says,

> By this all men will know that you are my disciples, if you love one another." (John 13:35)

As you submit to Him, the Spirit of the Lord Jesus, who came into your heart when you believed the gospel, will help you overcome sin and reflect His holy character.

> The Holy Spirit produces this kind of fruit in our lives: love, joy, peace, patience, kindness, goodness, faithfulness, gentleness, and self-control. (Galatians 5:22-23 NLT)

As a child of the King, you have a new purpose in life: to honor Him. You are His ambassador to a lost world. Represent Him well. One day you will see Him face to face, and then you "will be like him" (1 John 3:2). Until then, talk to Him at any time. Praise Him in every situation. Worship and serve Him with others who love Him and His Word. Study the Scriptures daily (start with *Luke*, *John*, *Acts*, and *Romans*). The Holy Spirit is your Teacher. The Bible is your spiritual food and weapon against Satan, who does not want you to think, speak, and act like Jesus. The more you meditate on the Scriptures the stronger you will become spiritually.

I love this word picture from the Psalms:

> As the deer pants for streams of water, so my soul pants for you, O God. (Psalm 42:1)

Can you say that?

The choice is yours.

Paul D. Bramsen
resources@rockintl.org

Bonus Features

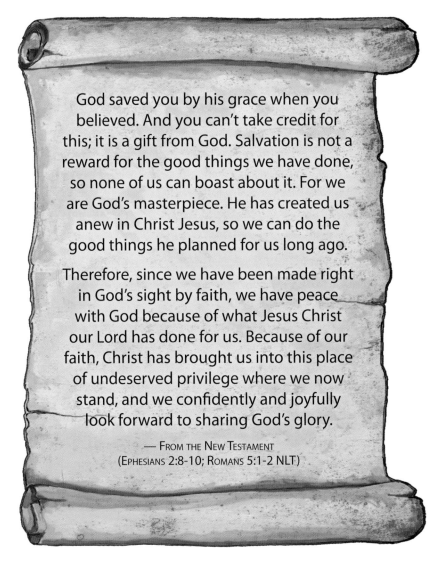

God saved you by his grace when you believed. And you can't take credit for this; it is a gift from God. Salvation is not a reward for the good things we have done, so none of us can boast about it. For we are God's masterpiece. He has created us anew in Christ Jesus, so we can do the good things he planned for us long ago.

Therefore, since we have been made right in God's sight by faith, we have peace with God because of what Jesus Christ our Lord has done for us. Because of our faith, Christ has brought us into this place of undeserved privilege where we now stand, and we confidently and joyfully look forward to sharing God's glory.

— FROM THE NEW TESTAMENT
(EPHESIANS 2:8-10; ROMANS 5:1-2 NLT)

REVIEW QUESTIONS • PART 1 • OLD TESTAMENT

This list provides a question or two for each of the 70 scenes. The answers are embedded in the text of each corresponding scene. Feel free to copy these pages for group studies. For more information visit: **www.one-god-one-message.com**

Scene number • question(s)

1 • The King of glory would take thousands of years to carry out His plans. What does this tell you about the King?

2 • Name the two main parts of the Bible. How are they different from each other?

3 • Do you believe the first words of Scripture (Genesis 1:1)? Why or why not?

4 • Even when God alone existed, He was never alone. What do you understand by this statement?

5 • What can we learn about God from the things He has made?

6 • Name some ways God made humans different from animals.

7 • Why did God not ask Adam if he wanted to live in Eden?

8 • What is sin? What did God say would happen to Adam if he disobeyed God's command? What is another word for death?

9 • Like Adam, Eve was created in the image of God. What does this mean?

10 • What is the best attraction in heaven?

11 • How did sin enter the universe?

12 • What did the LORD say would happen if man ate the fruit on the tree of the knowledge of good and evil? What did Satan say would happen?

13 • How did sin enter the human family?

14 • What was the first effect of sin? In what way did Adam and Eve's sin replace their honor with shame?

15 • In what way did Adam and Eve die the same day they sinned? How were they like a broken branch? (See also page 160.)

16 • Name some ways sin's curse has messed up the original creation.

17 • Why do you think God's secret plan included a Savior who would be the Offspring of a woman (having a human mother, but no human father)?

18 • What did God do to cover Adam and Eve's sin and shame?
How did God show them that He is a God of justice, mercy, and grace?

19 • Why did God put Adam and Eve out of the garden of Eden?

20 • How did Adam and Eve's sin affect their children? How
does it affect us and our families? (See also page 161.)

21 • What kind of a lamb would God accept to die in the sinner's place?

22 • What does *atonement* mean? Why did God require a death payment?

23 • What did God do with Abel's sin? What was wrong with Cain's offering?

24 • What does it mean to repent? What did God want Cain to do?
What did Cain do?

25 • What does the worldwide flood in Noah's time teach us
about the patience and judgment of God?

26 • What was the first thing Noah and his family
did after they came out of the ark?

27 • In what way does the tower of Babel illustrate false religion?

28 • What two big promises did the LORD make to
Abraham, if he would trust and follow the LORD?

29 • Why did God forgive Abraham and Sarah of
their sins and declare them righteous?

30 • What question did Abraham's son ask his father as
they walked up the mountain of sacrifice?

31 • God had promised to make Isaac the father of a new nation.
Since Abraham knew that God cannot lie, what did Abraham
think God would do after he sacrificed Isaac on the altar?

32 • Why did Abraham name the mountain *The LORD **Will** Provide*?
Did *the lamb* die in Abraham's son's place that day?

33 • How did the LORD fulfill the two big promises He had made to Abraham?

34 • If we try hard to obey God's commands, can we ever be good enough to
qualify to live with God in heaven? How are the Ten Commandments like a
mirror? In what way do the Commandments show us that we need a Savior?

35 • Why could animal sacrifices not take away the sin debt of the world?

36 • Choose one prophecy from the scroll and tell
how it pointed to the coming Savior.

37 • Why did God use four people (instead of just one person) to write the gospel story about Jesus?

38 • Why did the angel Gabriel call Jesus *the Son of God*?

39 • What does the name *Jesus* mean?

40 • What do you like best about the story of Jesus' birth?

41 • The angel told the shepherds, "A Savior has been born to you; he is Christ the Lord." Why would the Shepherds have been excited to hear this news?

42 • Was it right for the Magi to worship the child Jesus? Why or why not?

43 • In what way was Jesus different from other children?

44 • How was the prophet John's message different from the message of all previous prophets? Why do you think John pointed to Jesus and said, "Look, the Lamb of God, who takes away the sin of the world"?

45 • Look again at this scene and tell something you know from Scripture about the Spirit of God, the Son of God, and the Father in heaven.

46 • Why did Satan try to get Jesus to sin?

47 • After Jesus read from the scroll of the prophet Isaiah, He said, "Today this scripture is fulfilled in your hearing!" Why do you think this made His neighbors angry?

48 • How was Jesus *God's Arm* on earth? Why were the demons afraid of Jesus?

49 • After Jesus commanded the storm, "Silence! Be still!" the disciples said, "Who is this man? Even the wind and waves obey him!" Who do *you* think Jesus is?

50 • Why did the religious leaders accuse Jesus of blasphemy?

51 • Jesus said, "I am the resurrection and the life. He who believes in me will live, even though he dies." How do we know He spoke the truth?

52 • What did Jesus say to the people who came back the next day looking for more food?

53 • Review this scene and tell one thing Jesus said that surprised you.

54 • The prophets called the Messiah "the sun of righteousness." Jesus called Himself "the light of the world." How is Jesus the Messiah different from the prophets?

55 • What did the disciples think the Messiah should do? What did the Messiah come to do?

56 • Why did the Lord Jesus ride into Jerusalem on a lowly donkey instead of a mighty war-horse?

57 • Why could the religious leaders not trick Jesus into saying something wrong?

58 • Why did the high priest and Jewish rulers say that Jesus should be put to death?

59 • Why did Pilate condemn Jesus to death?

60 • The soldiers jammed a crown of thorns onto Jesus' head. Of what do the thorns remind us?

61 • How were Abraham's prophecies fulfilled by Jesus? How much are you worth to God?

62 • Two thieves were crucified next to Jesus. Today one is in hell (forever separated from the Lord) and one is in heaven (forever with the Lord). What made the difference?

63 • As the Lord Jesus hung on the cross in the darkness, what did the Father in heaven load on Him? Why did Jesus say, "It is finished"? Why did God rip the temple curtain?

64 • Did the disciples remember Jesus' promise to rise again? Did the wicked religious leaders remember His promise?

65 • What did the women find when they came to the tomb on Sunday morning? What did the religious leaders do about the empty tomb? If I trust completely in Jesus the Lamb of God who died for my sins and rose again, why do I not need to fear death?

66 • Why did the Lord Jesus tell the two travelers on the road to Emmaus that they were foolish?

67 • When the risen Savior appeared in the room, Thomas said to Him, "My Lord and my God!" Was Thomas right or wrong to call Jesus his Lord and his God? Why?

68 • What did Jesus tell His disciples to do after He returned to heaven?

69 • Who is the King of glory? What do you think about Him?

70 • When the King comes back, will you be happy or scared? Why?

ENDNOTES

Behind the Scenes: [1]While *Alice in Wonderland* is translated into nearly 200 languages, *the Holy Bible*, in whole or in part, is in more than 2,500 languages.

[2]The Bible is confirmed by archaeology, secular history, fulfilled prophecy, and the perfect consistency of a complex story written down over nearly two millennia.

Scene 2: [3]The King is not only the Creator and Sustainer of His universe, He is also the Author and Guardian of His book. The Dead Sea Scrolls confirm the Old Testament Scriptures of today to be the same Scriptures that existed before the time of Christ. The New Testament Scriptures are certified by thousands of ancient manuscripts, many dating to the early centuries after Christ. The popular claim that the original texts were tampered with and corrupted by men has no factual basis. See *One God One Message*, chapter 3. www.one-god-one-message.com

Scene 5: [4]For a deeper look into the attributes of God as seen in the six days of creation, see *One God One Message*, chapter 8.

Scene 6: [5]Since God is ONE, why does He say, "Let US make man in OUR image…"? The answer is embedded in His complex unity. In the Scriptures, the Hebrew word for "God" is *Elohim*, which is a plural noun. The word for "one" in the phrase "God is one" is *echad*, which can denote a compound unity. In eternity, before creating angels or man, God enjoyed fellowship within Himself—with His Word/Son and Holy Spirit. "How great is God—beyond our understanding!" (Prophet Job 36:26)

Scene 7: [6]The same chemical elements that make up the body are all present in the earth's dry dust. This fact was not acknowledged by science until recent times. While most scientists base their knowledge on observation and *theory* (man's ideas), the knowledge of those who believe the Bible is based on observation and *revelation* (God's Word).

Scene 11: [7]For more about the origin of Satan, see *One God One Message*, chapter 11.

Scene 16: [8]If the Lake of Fire, the place of eternal punishment, seems unjust or unreasonable to our minds, perhaps we have not yet understood the absolute holiness of God, the eternal nature of man, the gravity of sin, and the concept of eternity. The very word *eternity* overloads our mental capacities, since our frame of reference is time. Eternity is timeless. The God who created time is not bound by it (2 Peter 3:8-9). Eternity is not composed of years. Think of it as *an eternal now*. The moment sinners enter that inescapable realm, they will comprehend its solemn logic.

Scene 17: [9]To ransom (or redeem) means *to buy back by paying the required price*. In chapter 18 of *One God One Message* the author illustrates this with a story from his childhood:

As a boy growing up in California, I had a small dog. I would feed her, care for her, and play with her. She would follow me around and get excited when I returned home from school. But she had a fault. Sometimes she would wander into the neighborhood, though she always came back. Until one day.

I came home from school, but my dog wasn't there to welcome me. At bedtime, she was still nowhere to be found. The next day my father suggested I call the local animal shelter, a place that holds stray cats and dogs for a limited time. Unclaimed animals are euthanized.

I called the shelter. Yes, they had a small dog that met my description. The city's dog catcher had picked her up. My dog was helpless to save herself. If someone didn't come to her rescue, she would be put to death.

I went to the shelter. I was about to get my dog back! But the official at the front desk told me that if I wanted her back I must pay a penalty. It was against the law for a dog to run loose on the street.

I paid the required price and my dog was released. How glad she was to be out of that awful cage and back with the one who cared for her! She had been ransomed.

My boyhood experience in buying back my wayward dog gives us a faint idea of our own situation. As rebellious, condemned sinners, we have no way to rescue ourselves from the penalty of our sin, from the law of sin and death.

We need a Savior who can pay the ransom price.

Scene 23: [10]It is possible that God showed His approval of Abel's sacrifice by doing as He did as in the days of the prophets Moses, Solomon, and Elijah: "Fire blazed forth from the LORD's presence and consumed the burnt offering and the fat on the altar. (Leviticus 9:24; 2 Chronicles 7:1; 1 Kings 18:38).

Scene 30 & 61: [11]Moriah means *Chosen of the LORD*. It is the region where Jerusalem was later built. Today, Mount Moriah is the site where Solomon's temple once stood (2 Chronicles 3:1). Not far away, on the same mountain range is "the place called the Skull" (Luke 23:33).

Scene 36: [12]Fulfilled prophecy sets the Bible apart from all other books in the world. The prophets' prediction of future events, followed by their fulfilment in history, is one way God has validated His message. Only God can "make known the end from the beginning, from ancient times, what is still to come" (Isaiah 46:10). Jesus the Messiah said, "I am telling you now before it happens, so that when it does happen you will believe that I am He" (John 13:19). See *One God One Message*, chapter 5.

Scene 41: [13]Christ is the Greek word for the Hebrew word *Messiah*, meaning *The Chosen One*.

[14]The dating of events in history is based on the year Jesus Christ was born. For example, the prophet Abraham was born around 2000 BC (2,000 years *Before Christ* was born). This book (*King of Glory*) was written in AD 2011 (more than 2,000 years *After Christ* was born). AD is short for *Anno Domini*, Latin for *In the year of our Lord*. Many today use BCE (Before Common Era) and CE (Common Era) to remove Christ from the abbreviation, but the dividing point of history is still the birth of Jesus Christ.

Scene 43: [15]"'Isn't this the carpenter? Isn't this Mary's son and the brother of James, Joseph, Judas and Simon? Aren't his sisters here with us?' And they took offence at him." (Mark 6:3). Since Joseph was not Jesus' biological father, Jesus' was related to His brothers and sisters only on His mother's side. Jesus was the Son of God and Son of Man. See Endnote 19 (Scene 52).

Scenes 43 & 58: [16]Each year at the Passover Feast, the Jews remembered an event that had taken place in Moses' day when they were slaves in Egypt. Their ancestors had killed lambs and put the blood on the doorposts of their houses because God had said, "When I see the blood, I will pass over you" (Exodus 12:13). At midnight the LORD put to death the firstborn son in every home where there was no lamb's blood on the doorposts. God used this event to rescue His people from 400 years of slavery.

Scene 45: [17]This side of heaven, we will never fully understand God's tri-unity. After all, He is GOD. One thing we all understand, however, is the concept of something being three, yet one. Our world is filled with three-in-one unities: TIME: consisting of past, present, and future. SPACE: length, width, height. MAN: spirit, soul, body. ATOM: electrons, protons, neutrons. Our SUN is also a tri-unity. We call the celestial body *the sun*, its light *the sun*, and its heat *the sun*, yet the sun is *one*. So it is with the LORD who is Eternal Father, Eternal Son, and Eternal Holy Spirit. As the light and heat proceed from the sun, so the Son (Word) of God and Holy Spirit of God proceed from God, yet "the LORD is one" (Deuteronomy 6:4). See also Scene 4 and Endnote 5 (Scene 6). For more on God's complex unity and Jesus' human and divine nature, read *One God One Message*, chapters 9 and 17. Better yet, read the Gospel of John.

Scene 47: [18]Messiah means *The Chosen One* or, more literally, *The Anointed One*. In ancient times in the East, when a new king was inaugurated, a priest or prophet would pour a special anointing oil on his head to show that he was the new ruler of the kingdom. Jesus was not anointed by a man, but by the Holy Spirit Himself (see Scene 45).

Scene 52: [19]Jesus often referred to Himself as the Son of Man. He had always been the Son of God, but He became the Son of Man. As the Son of God He is the Word who was with God in the beginning (John 1:2; Genesis 1:3), but as the Son of Man He is the Word who became flesh, the One chosen by God to be the Savior-Judge-King of the world (John 1:14; Daniel 7:13-14).

Scene 56: [20]The Pharisees were members of a zealous Jewish sect. Some of them prayed six times a day, fasted three months a year, and gave ten percent of their income to the poor (Luke 18:9-14). But it was all an empty ritual. They were religious, but they did not know and love God.

Scene 68: [21]For believers in the Lord Jesus Christ, baptism is a way to declare their choice to follow Him. Being immersed in water does not take away sin. It symbolizes a person's identification with Jesus in His death, burial, and resurrection. Water baptism also pictures the end of the old life and the start of a new life in Christ.

[22]Not many days after the Son of God went up to heaven, the Spirit of God came down to live in the heart of every man, woman, and child who believed the gospel. The book of Acts in the New Testament records the exciting story about how the Holy Spirit gave the disciples power to reflect the character of Jesus and make His message known to the nations. God's way of salvation has not changed. If you make the choice to believe His message—that you are a sinner separated from a holy God and helpless to save yourself from the penalty of sin and that Jesus Christ took your punishment on the cross, was buried, and rose from the dead—then you too will receive the gift of the Holy Spirit. This means that the King of the universe Himself will come to live in your heart. He will become your new Master, Father, and Friend. The Scripture says, "And now you also have heard the truth, the Good News that God saves you. And when you believed in Christ, he identified you as his own by giving you the Holy Spirit, whom he promised long ago. The Spirit is God's guarantee that he will give us everything he promised and that he has purchased us to be his own people. This is just one more reason for us to praise our glorious God" (Ephesians 1:13-14 NLT). God is a big, wonderful King and He is going to have a big, wonderful family with Him throughout eternity. Will you be there?

GOING DEEPER

Like KING OF GLORY, ONE GOD ONE MESSAGE takes you on a journey into the Scriptures of the prophets, but in a deeper way as it compares the Bible's message with other worldviews. Questions left unanswered in KING OF GLORY (due to space limitations and a younger audience) are answered in ONE GOD ONE MESSAGE.

While KING OF GLORY takes less than three hours to read aloud, ONE GOD ONE MESSAGE takes about twelve hours.

Weaving together personal experiences, e-mails from skeptics, and a fresh retelling of history's most-told story, this book offers a framework for rethinking life's big questions.

- Author: P. D. Bramsen
- Illustrator: D. C. Bramsen
- Publisher: ROCK International
- Distributor: Independent Publishers Group
- ISBN 978-0979870606 (Third Edition, 2008)
- 432 pages.
- More than 30 illustrations.
- 150-question discussion guide.
- 271 Endnotes.
- Free downloads in Arabic, Albanian, Chinese, English, Farsi, French, Russian, Spanish, Turkish, Urdu, Indonesian …
- **www.one-god-one-message.com**

This book is a mine of truth; the writing style is unique; it is full of human interest.
    —William MacDonald, author of *Believer's Bible Commentary* and 80 other books

The e-mail excerpts assure the reader the author is not shying away from hard questions.
    — Vaughan, premed grad from South Africa

It reads like a detective story, which in a sense it is.
    — Theo, reader in Canada

After reading this book the logic in the Bible makes sense and clicks in my mind. It has created an interest in me to read the Bible.
    — Mohammed, Middle Eastern correspondent